Dedicated to:
My three sons

———————

WHAT
GENERATION
GAP???

WHAT GENER

"We now have a substantial number
of young people . . . willing to go to
any extreme to impose their will on
others. They have created unprecedented turmoil in our schools and
unless remedial steps are taken I have
no doubt that they will increase their
numbers. . . . We have seen this
develop in Japan, where first the
disruption was limited to part of the
universities, then extended to paralyze
whole institutions. . . ."

A Dialogue On America

TION GAP???

by James Louis Robertson

Photo shows Hiroshima University Administration Building after police routed extremist students who had occupied the building for six months in 1969.
—UPI PHOTO

published by

acropolis books

WASHINGTON, D. C. 20009

ACROPOLIS BOOKS
Colortone Building, 2400 17th St., N.W.
Washington, D. C. 20009

Printed in the United States of America by
Colortone Creative Graphics Inc., *Washington, D. C. 20009*

Type set in Sans and Bodoni
by Colortone Typographic Division, Inc.

Design by Design and Art Studio 2400, Inc.

Library of Congress Catalog Number 72-114036
Standard Book No. 87491-129-X

acknowledgement

I wish to express my deep gratitude to all my correspondents for the pleasure and stimulation their letters have provided, and especially to those who have consented to the use of their letters in a manner designed to help concerned people in their search for answers and solutions to some of the many questions and problems which confront us. I owe a heavy debt to my long time friend and associate, Mr. Reed J. Irvine, a strong believer in the value of freedom and the worth-while ness of preserving it; without his enthusiastic and constant prodding, as well as his helpful assistance, this project would never have gotten off the ground. In addition, my thanks to an old friend and schoolmate, Dr. Lawrence Keitt, and to my faithful and efficient secretary, Mrs. Dorothy Mooney, for whose voluntary abstention from watching clocks and calendars I shall ever be grateful. All of these people have given their assistance freely with no thought of monetary gain (as is true in my own case as well, for the royalties will be donated to a worthy charity). —J. L. R.

7

contents

introduction

RIFLE-TOTING STUDENTS LEAVE
WILLARD STRAIGHT HALL AT CORNELL

200 STUDENTS FIGHT COLUMBIA GUARDS

QUEENS STUDENTS ESCALATE PROTEST

STUDENTS ASSAIL FORDHAM R. O. T. C.

HEADLINES SUCH AS THESE BEGAN to appear in the daily
newspapers with alarming frequency in the early part of 1969. The
turmoil on the college campuses, which had erupted the previous
spring when students led by the revolutionary Students for a Democratic Society occupied buildings on the Columbia campus, appeared
to be increasing. The display of guns by the black students who took
over Willard Straight Hall at Cornell sent a shock wave across the
country. It was clearly no longer possible to shrug off the disturbances
at the colleges as youthful pranks, little more serious than the panty
raids of days gone by.

Rifle-toting students leave Willard Straight Hall at Cornell University.

This was one of the events on college campuses that shocked America in the spring of 1969.—UPI PHOTO

These developments were very much on my mind as I began thinking of what I would say in a talk I was scheduled to give in May, 1969. My audience was to be a group of bankers and businessmen in Omaha, Nebraska. There were many problems that were sure to be of concern to them. Inflationary price rises were on everyone's mind. The Federal Reserve System had been tightening the monetary screws to combat the inflation, and as a result interest rates were soaring to record levels. Banks, squeezed for funds, were borrowing heavily in Europe. The bankers were no doubt expecting me to say something on the pressing problems that confronted their industry.

However, as I read those headlines and the stories beneath them, the conviction grew that it was high time someone spoke out forcefully against the fallacious ideas that appeared to be at the root of the campus turmoil. It was clear to me that something was profoundly amiss in our educational system. It was clearly doing a fine job of technical education. We were turning out superior engineers, chemists, doctors, et cetera. But suddenly we seemed to have forgotten that one of the primary missions of education is to perpetuate the value system on which our civilization is based.

If we failed in that, we would deny our descendants their rightful heritage. The young people who were caught up in the wave of violent confrontation were being criticized, to be sure. There was much talk of legal action that might be taken to cope with misdeeds on the campuses. But it seemed to me that we of the older generation had a responsibility to do more than criticize and punish the young. We had a duty to educate them. We could not escape some of the blame for what was happening.

Men of affairs in our increasingly specialized age have tended to mind their own business and leave other matters up to those who were supposedly expert in them. But everyone of us is or should be concerned about the problem of keeping the fabric of our free society from coming apart at the seams. We are proud of the fact that we have a pluralistic society. For nearly two hundred years we have demonstrated that it is possible for people who have very different ethnic, cultural, religious, and economic backgrounds to live together in

13

harmony and cooperate for their mutual advancement. What has made this possible are the ideas and values that were agreed upon at the foundation of our country. These have been treasured and handed down from generation to generation.

In the spring of 1969 these ideas and values were under vigorous attack. The seams that have bound these diverse fabrics together were beginning to show signs of pulling apart. Important as the problems in inflation and tight money were, it seemed to me that in May, 1969, the most important thing that I or any other concerned citizen could do would be to focus attention on what was happening, to arouse our leading citizens to the danger confronting us. Those who love freedom cannot afford to leave the field to those strident voices who through ignorance or guile are trying to propel us down a road that can only result in the diminution or total loss of freedom.

For that reason, I stepped out of my role as a central banker and addressed my fellow citizens in my home state of Nebraska as a concerned citizen. My remarks were prepared in advance and released to the press in Washington as usual. My own concern with the problem was evidently not shared by those journalists in Washington who eagerly scan pronouncements of public officials with an eye to finding something sensational to put on the wire, some sign of controversy, or some hint of a change in official policy. No mention of the speech was carried by the wire services or the large eastern newspapers. One experienced newsman explained this by saying that I had ventured beyond the field of my expertise and what I had to say was therefore not newsworthy. He could not explain why a professor of biology who had ventured into the same area, only to justify the youth rebellion rather than criticize it, had been considered prime news copy only a few weeks earlier. Perhaps biologists are presumed to know more about political and moral philosophy than are public officials.

However, a few weeks later I picked up a copy of the *U. S. News and World Report*, and much to my surprise found that the editor had seen fit to publish my entire speech in the place usually reserved for his own editorial comment.

I was reminded of Mr. Justice Holmes' comment—in explaining

his lack of enthusiasm for reading daily newspapers—to the effect that if a news story was not good enough to find its way into a good periodical, it probably was not worth reading.

The public response was immediate. Letters began flooding my desk. Nearly all were commendatory and heartwarming. All were from concerned people. All were acknowledged, and some—those which raised serious questions—were answered as fully as time would permit. This was done because of (1) my belief that problems must be discussed openly, dispassionately, and fully if appropriate solutions are to be developed (they are not apt to come into being full-blown), and (2) my feeling that anyone concerned enough to take the time to write to me deserved a response.

One of those letters was from a young high school student in Great Neck, New York, Marc Machiz. It was lengthy and had been written by hand. It was addressed to the editor of the *U.S. News and World Report*, with a request that it be forwarded to me. I was impressed with the intelligence and sincerity of the writer. To me, he seemed to typify a large segment of our fine young people—earnest, idealistic, and intelligent, but weak in understanding of the basic facts and fundamental principles relating to economic and political problems. Marc's letter included a number of slogans and statements that cried out for critical examination. I felt impelled to reply to him as I would to one of my own sons if he had been similarly indoctrinated. As a courtesy, I sent a copy to Mr. David Lawrence, the editor of *U.S. News and World Report*, without any thought that it would be published. Much to my surprise, Mr. Lawrence published Marc's letter and my reply, verbatim, under the heading: "One Generation Speaks to Another."

This brought a new flood of mail to my office. Again most of it was laudatory, but this time there were more letters from those who were critical of my position or who wanted to raise additional questions. Many of them were from younger people, and I tried to respond to all of them, in much the same spirit that I had responded to Marc.

Many of the people who wrote to me suggested that both the original speech and the exchange with Marc Machiz should be distributed more widely. Some who had seen other parts of the correspondence expressed the view that the public interest would be served by publication of many of the other letters that I had received, together with my replies. It was suggested that this might help both the parents and their children restore meaningful communication.

Moved by the hope that this might be the case, I have drawn together in this book the original speech and a small portion of the correspondence, with only minor editing to correct spelling and to delete personal references which would be meaningful only to my correspondents and me. An effort has been made to obtain the approval of each correspondent to use his or her letter verbatim. In cases where consent has not been received, the correspondent has not been identified; where consent has been withheld, the incoming letter has not been included but the points or questions raised have been summarized to the extent needed to make the response relevant. Obviously both the incoming letters and my responses would have been more polished and better researched if they had been written with publication in mind, but hindsight editing for the sake of polish has not been employed. A few incoming letters are included without the responses, only to show the widespread interest in the dialogue evidencing concern by people of all ages and in all walks of life.

I should make clear that my desire it not to stifle dissent or discourage involvement by concerned people. After all, I was brought to Washington more than forty years ago by one of the greatest of our liberal dissenters, the late Senator George W. Norris, and my own role as a dissenter is fairly well known, at least in financial circles.

However, I see no virtue in dissent merely for the sake of dissent. We have a higher obligation to seek out and uphold Truth. Those who criticize and advocate the dissolution of our institutions on the basis of incorrect or inadequate knowledge and information are not entitled to glorification simply because they are in dissent. If they are in the wrong, there is nothing improper about saying so. I realize that it is not entirely popular in fashionable circles to believe that Truth is ascertainable. The modern intellectual has been conditioned to suspend judgment to the point where we are approaching the situation described by W. B. Yeats, when —

"The best lack all conviction
"While the worst are full of passionate intensity."

The best will not triumph if this is true.

We need not muzzle those who have declared war on the system of values and the basic ideas that enable our pluralistic society to function. But on the other hand, we had better not elevate them as models for our youth, as teachers, as spiritual counselors, or even entertainers, unless we have so little faith in our value system that we are content to see it destroyed or rendered inoperable.

And if we cannot agree on what Truth is, we should at least be able to agree that we cannot chart a sound course on the basis of misinformation and falsehoods.

We have many problems to face and resolve. Many sincere, idealistic people—young and old—have views with respect to them. It behooves all of us to listen to those views, try to understand them, sort out the good from the bad, work for the adoption of the best of them, and continuously work to make this world a better place to live— regardless of race, color or creed. This will not be easy, but all of us know that freedom doesn't come free.

part 1

the
challenge*

A TRUCK DRIVER was sitting all by himself at the counter of the
Neverclose Restaurant down by the depot in my home town, Broken
Bow, Nebraska. The waitress had just served him when three swagger-
ing, leather-jacketed motorcyclists—of the Hell's Angels type—rushed
in, apparently spoiling for a fight. One grabbed the hamburger off his
plate; another took a handful of his French fries; and the third picked
up his coffee and began to drink it. The trucker did not respond as one
might expect of a Nebraskan. Instead, he calmly rose, picked up his
check, walked to the front of the room, put the check and his half-
dollar on the cash register, and went out the door. The waitress
followed him to put the money in the till and stood watching out the
window as he drove off. When she returned, one of the cyclists said to
her: "Well, he's not much of a man is he?" She replied, "Nope. He's
not much of a truck driver either—he just ran over three motorcycles."

---

*Speech delivered at Omaha, Nebraska, May 22, 1969.

    The Nebraska newspapers reported the speech and several dailies subse-
quently printed the text, including the New Haven Register and the San
Francisco Chronicle.

Like the trucker's response, mine will be different, too—hopefully though without running over any motorcycles. As a central banker, I might be expected to talk about the awesome domestic and international financial problems which are the subject of my official concern. I am concerned about those problems, and especially the need to combat inflation hard enough and fast enough to keep it from getting out of hand. I will be glad to discuss those matters later, in response to questions, if first you will let me speak briefly, not as a central banker, but as a concerned citizen, about a matter which is or should be of deep concern to each and every citizen of this great land. I refer to the crisis that is manifest in the chaotic conditions that have developed in many of our institutions of higher learning, and even in some of our high schools.

I find myself increasingly troubled by these developments. It might be inaccurate to say that people are apathetic about it, but too many of us are seemingly content to be hand-wringers, head-shakers, and condemners.

This is not the way Americans typically respond to difficulties. We tend to be activists and problem solvers. Our motto when confronted with a difficulty is: "Don't just stand there; *do* something!" Today, we appear to have too many people, mostly young ones, who think of themselves as problem solvers and activists but who want to *undo* something. They want to undo and destroy what it has taken men centuries to build. They have an almost ferocious conviction of their own righteousness and wisdom. They see themselves as the only real devotees in the world of the true, the good, and the beautiful. But to those of us who have lived a little longer and acquired a little more knowledge, and a little more experience, what they seek is neither true, nor good, nor beautiful.

One of the advantages that age has over youth is that we have been in their position, but they have never been in ours. We know those fiery passions, that hot idealism, that unshakeable certainty that one has within his grasp the solutions to all the world's problems. But experience has taught us that reason is a better guide to action than passion, that beautiful dreams of the young idealists sometimes end up as bitter nightmares, and that those men who had the greatest certainty that they had the final solution to all problems have ended up portrayed in the history books as tyrants and enemies of mankind.

This is not to say that we should discourage the dreams of the idealists and the aspirations of our youth. Quite the opposite, we should encourage those dreams and aspirations and pay heed to the expressions of dissent which flow therefrom, for there is the source of orderly change and progress. But we must teach them what we taught their older brothers, what we ourselves were taught, and what our fathers were taught—that our wants and aspirations must be tempered to accommodate the legitimate wants and aspirations of others who live with us on this planet; that other people have rights and that these rights are embodied in laws that have been worked out over hundreds of years to make it possible for men to live together in some degree of harmony and to work for common ends; that these laws are our protection against others trampling on our rights; that if we ignore or destroy the law, we jeopardize our own liberty as well as the liberty of others.

We have recently seen a distinguished Harvard professor and Nobel Prize winner explain and justify the behavior of those who would destroy the law by saying in effect that these young people want something very badly and they have not been able to get it in any other way. This is very much like explaining and justifying the behavior of a child who throws a tantrum in a department store by saying that the youngster wanted a toy fire engine very badly and had no other way of getting it. Sensible parents know that children must be taught at an early age that throwing temper tantrums is not an acceptable way of getting what they want. This is done by punishing—not rewarding—those who engage in unacceptable conduct. Society must do the same. The good parent is not the permissive one who tolerates and encourages temper tantrums in children. The overwhelming majority of parents realize this and hence it is possible to walk through our department stores without having to step over the bodies of screaming children lying in the aisles pounding their fists upon the floor. Unfortunately, this is not true of our colleges, where mass teen-age temper tantrums have become a regular part of the campus scene.

The other day the Chief of Police of Los Angeles retired after a quarter of century of service and stated that he was about ready to write off a whole generation of young Americans because of their attitude toward authority. Now, we cannot afford to write off a whole generation of young Americans—not even its small minority about whom I am talking. Every generation plays a vital role in the process of keeping civilization alive. We cannot write off a generation if we hope to transmit to the generations to come the values that man has laboriously nurtured and protected over the centuries.

Our country has survived and prospered because of the ideas on which it was founded. People from all parts of the globe came here to live. They spoke a variety of languages and had widely disparate economic, social, and cultural backgrounds. Yet they succeeded in building a great nation. A nation is more than a collection of human beings who live in the same geographical area. To constitute a viable nation, these human beings must sense a community of interest, must share a common set of operational values. America's glory lies in the fact that it won voluntary acceptance of its values from men and women of widely different backgrounds. This was perhaps largely because so many were attracted to this wild country in its early days precisely because they were impressed by what we stood for. Many had fled from authoritarianism and tyranny, to live in a land that offered them both liberty and justice.

This has always been the kind of country that allowed wide latitude to its citizens in both speech and action. However, it was expected in return that the citizens would respect and support the institutions, laws, and customs that were essential to the survival of a society of this kind. It was expected, for example, that the citizens would accept the principle of majority rule, and obey the laws approved by the majority. It was expected that the majority would respect the constitutional safeguards erected to curb its power and safeguard the rights of minorities. It was expected that when the majority decided that the national interest led the country into conflict with a foreign enemy, all citizens, regardless of their personal views or national origin, would support and defend the United States. Thus it was that Nebraska's great statesman, Senator George W. Norris, after having vigorously opposed America's entry into the first World War, declared his unstinting support for the Commander-in-Chief once war was declared.

Underlying these operational principles were some commonly accepted moral values that helped bind the American people together. We shared a belief in the Judeo-Christian religious and ethical values—respect for truth, respect for human dignity, consideration of the rights of others, and a common conviction that man had a higher purpose in life than animalistic gratification of his sensual desires. It is true that we have made many mistakes and that our practices have not always matched our beliefs, but we have generally recognized the value of aspiring for more than we could hope to achieve. And we were generally understanding and tolerant of our human and social imperfections, knowing that it was vain to expect to build Utopia here on earth.

The ideas that made this nation what it has become—a beacon in a dark world—did not spring up overnight. They were not the product of any single individual. They grew and developed over centuries before they reached their present development here. These ideas will not die overnight, but what is transpiring at this moment in our country is a concerted effort to bring about their demise. The turmoil on the college campuses is but a symptom of it. A minority, but an articulate and activist minority of young people—young people who may be future teachers, writers, and political leaders—apparently have been persuaded that the cementing ideas that made this a great nation are false. Indeed, some of them deny that this nation has achieved anything praiseworthy.

These young people have a different set of ideas and ideals. They believe that freedom of expression for those with whom they disagree should not be tolerated. They believe that laws which are not to their liking should be ignored and flouted. They believe that their country is generally wrong in its disputes with foreign countries and hence they have no obligation to give it any support or to rise to its defense. They proclaim their respect for truth, but they show little interest in undertaking the kind of arduous and dispassionate search for facts that is essential if truth is to be found. They profess profound respect for the rights of all men, but they physically assault those whose opinions differ from their own, invade the privacy of their offices, rifle their files, and boastfully publish private correspondence of others to achieve some political advantage.

John W. Gardner, in his recent Godkin Lectures at Harvard, put it well when he said:

"Sad to say, it's fun to hate. . . . That is today's fashion. Rage and hate in a good cause! Be vicious for virtue, self-indulgent for higher purposes, dishonest in the service of a higher honesty."

But as he and many others have pointed out, it takes little imagination to visualize the kind of state these youthful revolutionaries would create if they had the power. Constitutional safeguards for the rights of even those who arrogate power unto themselves—let alone everyone else—would cease to exist. There would be no freedom of expression. Truth would be what the rulers believed, not what objective investigation might show. Personal privacy would disappear. The age of Orwell's Big Brother would be upon us, for the historic pattern of continuing *violent* protest is clear. First comes revolution, with the overthrow of the good along with the bad, followed by chaos, and finally by dictatorial control. Only then could the long, agonizing struggle to obtain the four freedoms begin anew.

Perhaps because of the obvious risk of losing so much for so little, some of us are tempted to say: "It can't happen here!" But it happened, in our lifetime—Russia, Italy, Germany, all of Eastern Europe, China, and Cuba. It could not happen here if we took greater pains to preserve and protect the operational values of our society. It will happen here if through carelessness we permit these values to be lost to that generation that some people are already prepared to write off.

We must appreciate that changes in basic ideas take place slowly, almost imperceptibly. What has happened on our college campuses is merely a reflection of an attack on our basic ideas that has been going on for many years. When the competing ideas begin to produce the kind of overt behavior we now observe, they have already secured a strong and dangerous foothold.

The question is, are we prepared to battle for the preservation of the ideas that made this country great? Do we believe in them enough to insist that they be transmitted to succeeding generations? Or will we—beset by doubts and uncertainty—decide that it is too much trouble to stave off the onslaught of the totalitarians?

Our survival as a free nation may well depend on our answer to this question: Is it too much to ask that our youth be taught—at school as well as at home—to value and respect the ideas that have given this country unexampled freedom as well as material abundance?

I, for one, do not think we price liberty too high when we ask that those who wish to enjoy it give their allegiance to the institutions and ideas that make it possible, even while seeking to change them through nonviolent dissent.

Edmund Burke once said, "The people never give up their liberty but under some delusion." What is the source of the delusion that has led so many of our brightest youth to place liberty in jeopardy? If we are to be more than hand-wringers and head-shakers, we must probe for the answer to that question. For me, it is difficult to escape the conclusion that the finger points at those of us who have neglected the education of our youth, and especially at those who condone, forgive, and even justify violations of law and outrageous assaults upon the rights of others.

Would that every parent and teacher take upon himself the responsibility of conveying to the young the wisdom contained in Burke's words:

"Men are qualified for civil liberty in exact proportion to their disposition to put chains upon their own appetites; in proportion as their love of justice is above their rapacity; in proportion as their soundness and sobriety of understanding is above their vanity and presumption; in proportion as they are more disposed to listen to the counsels of the wise and the good, in preference to the flattery of knaves."

25

part 2

echoes

THE LETTERS THAT POURED IN commenting on the foregoing speech were overwhelmingly favorable, echoing my views or praising them. Some raised interesting points.

For example, Mr. Rafael A. Catasus of Richmond, Virginia, had this to say:

"As a Cuban by birth who lived in Cuba up to 1961 I witnessed and experienced (a more appropriate word would be perhaps, suffered) more than one episode in the long tragedy of my unfortunate native-country.

"Because of that I am probably in a better position than the average U.S. citizen to understand your concern, which I share with you completely, and to appreciate the soundness and wisdom of the remedy you suggest.

"I had long been expecting a statement such as yours and now that I have read it, so eloquently expressed and by a man in a position so responsible and influential as yours, I cannot help but feel better and hope that your advice be put into practice for the good of us all."

Another correspondent, Mr. Benjamin Ginzburg of Arlington,

27

Virginia, commented on the surprise he felt at finding a banker discourse on morality. He wrote:

"My bewilderment at beholding a speech of a moralist coming from the mouth of a banker was a little like the bewilderment felt by a British writer after the Six Day Israeli-Arab War. 'Who would have thought a generation ago,' he wrote, 'that the Jews would become a military people and the Japanese a trading people!'"

Mr. Ginzburg urged me to consider taking to the college lecture circuit, saying, "It is the academic people who need your words of wisdom more than your fellow bankers." He added this sage comment:

"It is imperative to restore moral common sense in America, and stop reacting to outrages as if they were the expression of rational and moral grievances. We must stop explaining human behavior as determined purely by biological and sociological forces, and recognize that what distinguishes man from a Pavlovian dog is precisely his capacity to listen to the call of moral values and progressively develop laws and institutions which embody these values."

A young man, Michael Workland of Spokane, Washington, said this:

"Being a young man myself (28 yrs.), I too am deeply concerned with the present turmoil and undoing of our basic rights and ideals. It seems there is no 'sense of direction.' Without a sense of direction we have what T. S. Eliot calls the 'wasteland.' This absence of unity in our civilization makes our country a land of dead ideals, dead souls, dead cities. Youth must bear in mind that with every right goes a serious 'obligation.'

"It is through justice that our liberty is assured. To flout the law will abolish that hard-fought liberty! Youth should dedicate their energies and ideals towards serving as the rivets of the community in the cause of peace and unity."

Mr. Wilson C. Lucom of Bethesda, Maryland, wrote to ask why we had failed to instill in the younger generation a firm faith in the philosophy that had made America great. He asked how we might rectify the situation, and suggested that a White House Conference to ponder these questions might be in order.

I tried to provide some answers to the important questions raised by Mr. Lucom in the following letter:

June 16, 1969

Dear Mr. Lucom:

I certainly agree with you that it is important that we devote some time and effort to analyzing the causes of our failures and the remedies for them. Your suggestion that this would be an appropriate subject for a White House conference is an interesting one. I am not sure that we are ready for that, however, since it does not appear that there is as yet adequate agreement in the educational community on the nature of the problem. The first step will probably have to be to persuade our academic leaders that we must uphold a system of operational values if we are to retain our national integrity.

Indeed, I think this is one of the answers to your question about the reasons for our failure. Parents, educators, clergy, and those who operate our mass media have too often failed to see clearly that it is important to agree on fundamental operational values and then cooperate in transmitting these to the younger generation. We have almost made the right of dissent the supreme value, forgetting that we have come as far as we have not because we permitted unlimited dissent, but because we obtained near universal agreement on certain fundamentals. This was possible partly because nearly all of our people shared a similar religious heritage and there was no significant disagreement with the basic Judeo-Christian ethical teaching. This was powerfully reinforced with our educational system which inculcated belief in our basic political philosophy and encouraged love of country.

Unfortunately, the support that our value system has had from both the churches and the schools has been eroded simultaneously. This has had profound repercussions in other

29

areas. Nowhere has the impact been greater than in the communications media. The writers, editors and broadcasters who determine what we will read and what we will see on television are almost all the products of our educational institutions. The failure of those institutions to transmit respect for our traditional values bears fruit in the mass media, which seem increasingly to lose sight of the importance of maintaining high standards of accuracy, taste and good judgment.

The individual parent is left in a difficult situation. We may be determined to pass our own values on to our young, but all too often this is frustrated by the powerful influences that sow doubt and confusion, if nothing else.

What can be done?

It seems obvious to me that those of us who are not professional educators must take greater interest in what is happening in our schools and colleges. I think we should press for greater emphasis in the school on moral discipline and training. This has been one of the traditional roles of education, but it has tended to be pushed aside in recent decades. This is feasible, since education is largely under public control and educators are presumably responsive to the wishes of the public. However, it will only prosper if high level public officials become convinced of its need and press for action.

For this to be accomplished, there will first have to be understanding of the basic principle that human behavior is rooted in ideas. When individuals singly or in groups behave well or badly, the explanation will generally be found in the complex pattern of ideas that governs their conduct. If we want to influence conduct, minimizing that which is socially destructive, then we must think in terms of influencing the ideas that give rise to such conduct. This is why traditionally education was largely concerned with teaching ideas conducive to the preservation of moral standards.

If we accept this principle, we can then apply it appropriately in reformulating educational policies. We should also consider its implications for our mass media. The notion that the Constitution does not permit our society to in any way limit what is printed or disseminated over the air waves must be rooted in the notion that the articulation of ideas exercises no influence on human conduct. The authors of the Constitution did not subscribe to that notion, and throughout history a distinction has been drawn between liberty and license. It is always difficult to say precisely where the line between the two must be drawn, but the deplorable breakdown of respect for law that we see around us today is a clear indication that it has been a mistake to erase the line altogether.

However, I should add that I think a great deal can be done by persuading those in the media to put their own house in better order by establishing codes, such as the now defunct moving picture code, which prescribe standards of conduct. For example, a great deal of beneficial influence could be exerted by a nongovernmental body designed to prod the press into maintaining higher standards of accuracy, if nothing else. The press, and I include in that term radio and TV news, is currently suffering from a serious credibility gap of its own, occasioned by distorted reporting that in some cases has appeared to be deliberate. Perhaps if the press were prodded into observing the traditional journalistic standards of accuracy, it might also improve in taste and judgment.

These thoughts are perhaps not as specific as might be desired, but there is little hope of making progress on soundly conceived specific proposals unless we can first obtain substantial agreement on fundamental principles. I hope that you and other like-minded citizens will do what you can to bring about such agreement. I shall continue to do what I can.

Sincerely

J. L. Robertson

One of the letters that particularly touched me came from Margaret I. French, of Iowa City, Iowa, who said she had graduated from college some sixty years ago. What impressed me was not that she agreed with my views, but that at her advanced age she asked, "What quiet, unobtrusive thing could I do for my country?"

This was my reply:

June 11, 1969

Dear Mrs. French:

I have received many nice letters commenting on my talk, but yours is the only one that has posed the question: What can I do for my country?

It moves me that you should raise this question. People in retirement too often take the position that they are too old and too tired to make any contribution to the solution to the problems currently bedeviling us. I am sure, therefore, that with your spirit you are already making a contribution, for if nothing else, you set an example for the rest of us to emulate, and I am sure that this inspires those who know you.

It is difficult for me to indicate specific things that you might do, not knowing any of the details of your situation. You are evidently keeping abreast of developments and are in a position to comment on them in an informed manner. The fact that you have written to me suggests that you are disposed to do so.

Edmund Burke once warned that the world has a tendency to be impressed by a few noisily chirping crickets while ignoring thousands of cattle standing under the oaks silently chewing their cuds. He said the British people were like the sturdy but silent cattle, and that one should not take the racket caused by a few noisy "crickets" as being indicative of their feelings. What this suggests to me is that it would be well for more of us to articulate our feelings on important issues of the day, to make sure that the "crickets" do not give the wrong impression.

One way to do this is to do what you did in writing to me.

This gives encouragement to those who speak for you. Another is to communicate with those who run our newspapers, magazines, and radio and TV facilities. These people are very important, because it is they who can amplify or muffle what any of us has to say. The publicity these same media have given in recent years to the statements made by advocates of violence and lawlessness, making them into nationally known figures, is indicative of their power to amplify the chirping of the crickets until it sounds like a roar.

My suggestion is that you, and others like you, lose no opportunity to make your views and your wants known to those who control the various organs of communication in this country. If you feel that the news you are getting over radio, TV, or in the newspapers builds up those who want to tear our country down, write to the management telling them how you feel.

Of course, it is much better to comment on specific cases than it is to write in general terms. It is particularly important, in my view, to ask for correction when factual errors are made in reporting the news. Herbert Bayard Swope once said, "The first duty of the press is to be accurate. If it is accurate, it follows that it will be fair." Most journalists in this country have been trained to respect accuracy, but perhaps there are some who deliberately "shape the news" in order to try to influence the public reaction. We need to guard against such distortions. Individual citizens who are well informed can do a great deal in this area, although I am inclined to think that a private organization devoted to prodding the communications media to uphold the highest standards of accuracy is what we really need.

Thank you for your kind words. I hope that this response will provide you with some useful guidance.

Sincerely,

J. L. Robertson

Not all of the response to the speech was favorable. And not all the critics were members of the younger generation.

A New Orleans businessman, W. T. Freeland, wrote to David Lawrence, editor of *U. S. News and World Report,* bitterly scoring our monetary and banking system. He suggested that we could not expect our children to accept our teachings, have faith and behave as long as we maintained a system that permitted inflation.

I did not accept Mr. Freeland's challenge to justify our banking system, since that is a fit subject for a book, not a letter. But I did think it worth while to suggest that things were not quite as black as Mr. Freeland seemed to think. Here is his letter and my reply:

Dear Mr. Lawrence:

I just read the speech of Mr. James L. Robertson in no less prestigious place than **your** editorial page.

I share the same concerns and expressed values, but I'm wondering if Mr. Robertson is sincere, or, a con artist.

When we as a nation are living so many lies, how can we expect a younger generation to blindly accept our teachings, have faith, and behave? If I tell my children to work hard, be honest, save their money, and some day they will arrive, what will they think of me when they find that their store of value (money) is lefthandedly confiscated by inflation caused by the government and banking system, and that whereas they must work hard for their money, the banking system has only to create money with pen and ink. How can I tell them the constitution has meaning when the fundamental right to own gold is denied them? How can I tell them this is the land of freedom when to earn a living for themselves they must also pay about 50 per cent of their earnings in taxes, which means they are forced to work 50 per cent for this nebulous thing called government? The definition of slavery being forced servitude, then they are 50 per cent slave and may soon be 80 to 90 per cent slave. When they can be forced to serve involuntarily in the armed forces, isn't this forced servitude too?

34

I personally am afraid our money system is on the verge of collapse, which will bring untold suffering and chaos to innocent people. I would like to refer you to "A Primer on Money," "Money Facts" and "The ABCs of America's Money System" all available from U. S. Government Printing Office. Also, "Death of the Dollar" by William F. Rickenbacker, Arlington House, New Rochelle, New York, "What Has Government Done to Our Money" by Murray N. Rothbard, Pine Tree Press, Box 158, Larkspur, Colorado 80118. Dr. Ludwig Von Mises on "Current Monetary Problems," published by The Constitutional Alliance, 815 Monroe Avenue, N.W., Grand Rapids, Michigan 49502—40 cents. "Money Creators" available from OMNI Publications, Box 216, Hawthorne, California, and many others.

We need to clean up our sorry state of affairs before we ask the kids to behave in spite of us. Perhaps their misbehavior is the only thing that will force us to do it. If they can only feel that things are going to hell, can we blame them for taking a free ride as long as they can? We are beginning to reap the wages of false premises (socialism and false capitalism) and are prescribing all kinds of quack remedies to perpetuate them.

If you, or, Mr. Robertson can justify the banking system we have, I would be happy to have my faith restored.

Sincerely,
W. T. Freeland
New Orleans, Louisiana

June 17, 1969

Dear Mr. Freeland:

Mr. David Lawrence has forwarded to me a copy of your letter of June 7, commenting on my talk on campus turmoil.

I regret that we have not been able to maintain here in the United States, or anywhere else in the world, a completely inflation-free economy. However, even though our own performance has been something less than perfect, I think we can take some satisfaction from the knowledge that no major country has really done any better than we have over the long run.

I do not expect to find perfection on this earth in anything, especially in arrangements governing human affairs. But even if we were to attain what you or I might regard as perfection, I am sure that there would be many others who would find the results far from satisfactory.

One of the points that I tried to make in my talk is that it is necessary for all of us to compromise and settle for something less than what we might regard as ideal in order for us to live harmoniously in a democratic society. I do not want the student extremists imposing their ideas on our society by force, disregarding the desires of most of the people. I believe that it would be equally wrong for anyone else to impose his ideas by force, even though I might happen to think some of his ideas have validity. One of the things we have presumably agreed upon is that we will accept the will of the majority, and we will leave the door open for changes in opinion by reasoning and persuasion.

As you have noted in your letter, there are many articulate people in this country who have published criticisms of our system of money and banking and of our monetary policies. If and when these critics are able to persuade a majority of the people that their position is correct, we will no doubt see some fundamental changes in our system and in our policies. However, as long as the majority do not accept the arguments of the critics, as long as they elect to support existing programs and policies, I think that the elected representatives of the people and those that they appoint to administer the various agencies of government have an obligation to carry out those programs and policies.

I do not think you will be doing your children any favor if you advise them to refuse to support our democratic system of government because it has produced some results which are distasteful to you. As Churchill said, it is undoubtedly the worst form of government—except for all others.

I submit that a broader view of matters would suggest that you tell your children that those who have worked hard, saved their money and invested it wisely have certainly prospered in spite of inflation and high taxes. Despite all the poor-mouthing that we hear, this is certainly the most affluent society the world has ever known. I am much more concerned about our spiritual poverty than I am about the material hardships imposed by inflation and high taxes. Never before in history has there been a society with so much material abundance that one of its great problems was to find space to dispose of its waste materials. I am not at all sure that our greatest problem right now is to find more ways of expanding production and consumption of manufactured goods. We have been doing quite well at that. I am inclined to think that one of our biggest problems is to find better ways of developing human beings who can live together in reasonable harmony, respecting each other's persons and property, tolerating differences of opinion, but insisting on the rule of law.

I will not endeavor to restore your faith in the banking system, any more than I will endeavor to persuade the Students for a Democratic Society types that every businessman is not a filthy imperialistic exploiter. I would suggest to you, as I would to them, that before you recommend destroying the system, you examine carefully the actual working models of the alternatives to find one that functions more satisfactorily. Arguments based on actual experience are far more effective and convincing than those that depend entirely on comparison of the *status quo* with some theoretical model of perfection.

I thank you for giving me the benefit of your views. I hope that you will join with me in urging that those who want to improve our admittedly imperfect society do so through methods that are consistent with our democratic institutions.

Sincerely,

J. L. Robertson

part 3

reverberations

ONE OF THE CRITICAL COMMENTS on my talk produced some strong reverberations. Marc Machiz, a young high school student of Great Neck, New York, wrote to David Lawrence, the editor of *U. S. News and World Report*, saying that he felt that America was on fundamentally the wrong course and that its institutions did not merit support, but the most effective resistance that could be provided. He undertook to spell out in considerable detail why my defense of American institutions was wrong.

I was impressed by Marc's letter. Not that I found his arguments at all convincing. Quite the contrary. I was impressed by the fact that the author was obviously a highly intelligent and very idealistic young man, who was enough concerned about his country that he would take the trouble to explain why he thought it was in need of drastic reform or revolution. I had no doubt that the ideas he expressed with great conviction and sincerity had been inspired by someone older, perhaps a teacher, who had not only failed in the important task of explaining the essence of our country's freedom-loving, democratic philosophy, but who had planted ideas that might sound superficially noble, but which contained the seeds of totalitarianism.

39

I did not know Marc Machiz. But I felt that he typified many of the most intelligent and most idealistic members of our younger generation. He was one of those that some adults would write off as a lost cause, because he described himself as a "radical." To me, he symbolized my generation's failure to properly inculcate in many of our youngsters a thorough understanding of the ideas and principles that made America the hope of the world.

I resolved, therefore, to try to do my bit to see if I could communicate across the generation gap to this one young man. I wrote a detailed reply to Marc, trying to answer the major criticisms of America and its institutions that he had voiced. As a courtesy, I sent a copy of my reply to David Lawrence.

Much to my surprise, and I am sure to Marc's, his letter and my reply blossomed forth in the July 7, 1969 issue of *U. S. News and World Report* under the title, "One Generation Speaks to Another."

Marc's letter was as follows:

Sirs:

I read with interest the speech by James L. Robertson in your issue of June 9. It was one of the few honest, well-reasoned defenses of the establishment position I have come across, and as such requires an equally unemotional, well-reasoned reply. It is with a disturbing sense of my own inadequacy that I will attempt to supply one.

I am a high school student with "radical" beliefs. I believe that America today is fundamentally on the wrong course and that therefore its institutions do not merit support but rather the most effective resistance that can be provided. Here I differ from many or most of my radical counterparts in that I believe that nonviolent disobedience is ultimately more effective than violence. Because of this I am more acceptable to the establishment than, say SDS (Students for a Democratic Society.).

However, the difference between myself and others is merely one of tactics: I simply believe that the power

40

structure can be dismantled more effectively with non-violence. However, my goals and views of American society are essentially the same as my more-violent counterparts.

The basic underlying assumptions of James L. Robertson's speech were that the values upon which American society has rested are good and, further, that these values, operating through our institutions, are working toward good ends. These assumptions—considered almost axiomatic by many—need re-examining.

American society has always been materialistic. This basic materialism has manifested itself in many ways—some good, some bad. Historian Richard Hofstader, in "The American Political Tradition," has said that ours is "a democracy in cupidity rather than a democracy of fraternity." The idea that everyone is entitled to what is his and a chance to obtain more is the underlying principle behind American democracy.

The growth of democracy is one of the few—if not the only—totally good consequences of American materialism. To balance it we are forced to live in a society which places property rights above personal rights and freedoms. The most recent and graphic illustration of this is the "people's park" incident at Berkeley.

It is not surprising that the best defense of the established order should come from a central banker.

In the past our institutions—based on democracy but, even more fundamentally, on property rights and rights of opportunity—have managed to adjust to changing social and economic considerations. It was accomplished with relative ease in Jackson's time, with bumbling ineptness and neglect at the time of the "robber barons," and purely by the lucky circumstance of a war at the time of the Depression.

But now the challenge presented by affluence—which (economist J. Kenneth) Gailbraith wrote about in '58—and the black revolution have shown American institutions to be totally inadequate. The circumstances which took shape in the '50s, and have come to fruition in the '60s, are demonstrating every day that our institutions don't have the capability to adjust.

This is why so many young people are frustrated to the point of violence.

Rather than adjusting, American institutions have taken the defensive—e.g., Chicago.

Nixon's black capitalism and even Johnson's antipoverty program have proven themselves ineffectual.

In the midst of our affluence, millions starve because Americans believe that, once you have property, it is sacred—no matter that your neighbor starves and lives with rats.

American corporations exploit foreign labor and resources in Latin America, and we wonder why Rockefeller—the symbol of American business success—is greeted by violent demonstrations there.

Here in my home town, property owners—terrified that "ghetto" dwellers might ask for or demand their fair share—turn out in record numbers at the polls to reject the busing in of 60 to 200 elementary school students from Queens.

From my vantage point, we are confronted with a worn-out set of values. For once, our underlying values are in direct conflict with the sort of institutional change required by political and socio-economic circumstance, and the youth of today find themselves confronted with a majority firm in the conviction that the old values remain valid.

The question asked at this point is: How can we, as professed "liberals," advocate defying the will of the majority? We are accused of being anti-democratic and totalitarian.

One can answer by saying that the right of the black man to eat and obtain an education; the right of foreigners to be free of American corporate domination; the right of the individual not to kill or participate in institutions that will lead to the death of others if he feels it immoral, as declared at Nuremberg; the right to real freedom of expression and information in our educational institutions; the right to freedom from invasion of privacy by our governmental institutions—all of these rights are higher, of more value and more worthy of defense—to death, if need be—than the right of the majority to deny them.

We have reached a point in our development when we must replace our "democracy in cupidity" with a "democracy of fraternity," and when human rights must be placed above both property and majority rights.

We have reached a turning point. If we cannot see that it has been reached, God help us all.

Respectfully yours,
Marc Machiz

This was my reply:

Dear Marc:

Mr. David Lawrence has forwarded to me your very well-written letter commenting on my remarks on the turmoil on our campuses. Since you have taken the time and trouble to put down your views thoughtfully and dispassionately, I would like to give you my own reaction to the case you make. I want to comment on some of your key statements from the standpoint of their factual accuracy.

1. **"American society has always been materialistic."** If this means that Americans, like human beings the world over, have always been preoccupied with supplying themselves with food, clothing, and shelter, I agree. Man must of necessity supply his material requirements if he is to survive.

If, however, you mean to imply that Americans have been "exclusively" concerned with the accumulation of

43

material wealth and have, in comparison with other peoples, neglected the development of spiritual and esthetic achievements, I have to differ.

Our country was initially settled, in part, by dissenters who came here not because life pioneering in the American wilderness was easier and more materially rewarding than it was in Europe but because they found here greater freedom to realize their spiritual needs.

I think if you will probe into American history and study the sacrifices that have been made for idealistic goals—whether by the early settlers in the colonies, those who fought for independence, those who gave their lives in the Civil War, those who fought in World Wars I and II to resist the authoritarian and totalitarian movements in Europe and Asia—you may conclude that Americans, perhaps more than any nation in history, have been prone to sacrifice for great ideals.

I realize that there is a school of historians who seek to debunk all of this and would have you believe that behind every noble cause there has been a greedy motive. Charles A. Beard, the famous historian, was one of the popularizers of this idea, having written in his younger years a book called "An Economic Interpretation of the Constitution of the United States." This purported to show that the men who drafted and secured the adoption of our Constitution were motivated entirely by selfish economic interests. Charles Beard himself later rejected this theory, but it has nevertheless lived on.

This base view of man's motivations is plausible only when applied to people that we do not personally know. We all know from our own experience that there are many things we do that are unselfish. We know that our relatives and friends frequently sacrifice their own personal interests for the sake of others. What arrogance it is to assume that those whom we do not personally know, especially the great men of history, have been motivated only by the desire for personal gain!

I commend to your attention a new book by Milovan Djilas called "The Unperfect Society" in which he discusses how he came to realize the falsity of this concept which had been an essential ingredient of his faith as a Marxist. Condemned to prison for having written his scathing indictment of the Communist societies of Eastern Europe, Djilas asked himself how the Marxian theory of economic determinism could explain his own conduct—his sacrificing of his position of power and privilege as Vice President of Yugoslavia in order to expose what he considered to be error and injustice. He concluded that men were moved by ideas—not exclusively by selfish, material interests.

2. **"The growth of democracy is one of the few—if not the only—totally good consequences of American materialism."** The growth of democracy is not a consequence of materialism but a consequence of man's thinking about ideal forms of political organization. It has taken centuries for the Western world to achieve the present degree of success in the operation of democratic institutions.

It would, in my view, be more accurate to attribute America's economic progress to the fact that we have had a smoothly functioning democratic form of government that has encouraged individual initiative, enterprise, saving and investment. Men have been assured that they and their descendants could enjoy the fruits of their labor—that it would not be artibrarily sequestered by a capricious ruler or by private parties who could, with impunity, disregard the law.

The less-developed countries of the world have learned or are currently learning that their own economic progress depends on developing similar conditions. For nearly two decades many of them were enamored of the idea that they could lift themselves by their bootstraps by means which penalized private initiative and enterprise, denied or seriously impeded the right to earn profits and acquire

Machiz: *". . . we are forced to live in a society that placed property rights above personal rights and freedoms."*

Robertson: *". . . we erect no Berlin Wall around the United States."*

The photo shows workers under an armed guard making repairs in the Berlin Wall, created by the communists in 1961 to keep East Berliners from fleeing to the West.

—COURTESY: GERMAN INFORMATION CENTER

property, and discouraged saving and investment. They have found to their sorrow that these methods are not conducive to satisfactory economic development. And economic development—an increase in material abundance, if you will—is something they very much want.

I should note that an increase in material abundance produces many good consequences. Our society does not require that anyone participate in the consumption of most of the vast array of goods and services, such as higher education, medical care, symphony concerts, etc., and anyone who so desires may freely elect to live primitively if he so desires. If he cannot find sufficiently primitive conditions here in the United States, he is free to emigrate to a country where material abundance is lacking and where he can struggle unaided against nature. The fact that few elect to do so indicates that the overwhelming majority of people find material well-being more of a blessing than a curse.

3. "We are forced to live in a society which places property rights above personal rights and freedoms." First, let me point out that we erect no Berlin Wall around the United States. There is no off-limits zone around our borders—as there is in the Soviet Union—which can be entered at the risk of one's life by anyone desiring exit from the country. Emigration is free and unrestricted, and thus it is untrue to say that anyone is "forced" to live in our society. On the contrary, one is free to move to a society that satisfies him better if he can find one. This you will no doubt concede.

But what about the cliché that our society places property rights above personal rights? The right to own and control property is a personal right and one of the most important that we enjoy. What you really mean, I suspect, is that the personal right to own and control property is placed above other personal rights. It is generally recognized that there have to be limitations on personal rights. My right to swing my fist ends where your nose begins. If this were not the case, your personal right to be safe from intimidation would not be worth much.

Thus your right to own property would not be worth much if the law did not prevent others from trespassing on your property against your will. This may curb the right of others to freedom of movement, but that is one of the compromises necessary to enable men to live together in harmony. This is part of the body of law that has been worked out laboriously over the centuries.

The right to own and control property is not, of course, absolute. The state exercises the right of eminent domain and may, under due legal process, deprive one of his real property to carry out public purposes, provided it pays just compensation.

The power to tax is also the right of the society to take part of one's individual property in order to pay for governmental services. We have increasingly imposed what are known as transfer taxes, which take one man's property in the form of taxes and use it for the benefit of others, such as those who are on welfare.

Society has decided that the personal right to property can be legitimately curtailed to the extent necessary to provide support to those who are unable to support themselves. As you know and as you will come to appreciate better when you yourself are a taxpayer, the burden of taxation is rather heavy and a substantial part of the tax revenue is used to pay for services which may not be of any direct benefit to the person or corporation that pays the taxes.

Let me offer a little vignette that may help you understand why men of "liberal" views have always placed high value on the right not to be deprived of one's property capriciously.

Let us assume that you find a job this summer, work hard and save $500. You use this money to buy a used car, and one of the first things you do after you get the car is to take your girl to the movies, parking the car in a pay lot. When you come out of the movie, your car is not in the lot. The attendant explains that a student from Nigeria came along and took your car.

You ask why he let him get away with it, and he explains that the student told him that he needed a car very badly to commute to his university. He obtained only a very small allowance from home and could not afford to buy a car. Being a foreigner, he was not able to get a job to earn money here. The attendant says that he was convinced that the Nigerian student needed the car more than you did and he therefore let him have it. When you protest he says: "Are you the kind of person who would place property rights above human rights?"

If you were true to your philosophy, you would have to admit that he had a valid point, and I suppose you would drop the matter. You might wonder, however, what point there was in your working hard to earn money to buy a car if you were constantly faced with the possibility that someone might take it away from you on the grounds that his need was greater than yours.

Unless property rights are reasonably secure, man's incentive to work, save and invest is likely to be weakened and economic progress will be slowed. What is more— tensions and conflict will arise, since there are not many people who would take your broadminded attitude and willingly give up to the first claimant the things they had sweated hard to obtain for their own use and enjoyment.

4. **"The most recent and graphic illustration of this (the placing of the right of personal property above other personal rights) is the 'people's park' incident at Berkeley."** I do not know all of the details of this incident, but I notice that "The New York Times" of June 14, 1969, quotes Governor Reagan of California as saying that Chancellor Roger W. Heyns of the

Berkeley campus had repeatedly expressed willingness to discuss the "people's park development" with "squatters" prior to erecting a fence around the tract. "The Times" states: "But at no time," the Governor added, "did the 'squatters' designate a committee with which he could negotiate." The Governor pointed out that the leaders of the demonstration had subsequently issued a 13-point manifesto which included these points:

"We will shatter the myth that the University of California is a sacred institution with a special right to exist."

"We will demand a direct contribution from business, including Berkeley's biggest business—the university—to the community until a nation-wide assault on big business is successful."

"We will protect and expand our drug culture."

I wonder if it is not possible that the confrontation over the "people's park" was engineered for political reasons somewhat akin to those that motivated the SDS in creating an issue over Columbia University's plan to build a gymnasium. Are you sure that it would be desirable to have a system in which the use to which property was put was determined by according primacy to "squatters' rights"?

5. **"The challenge presented by affluence . . . and the black revolution have shown American institutions to be totally inadequate. . . . Our institutions don't have the capability to adjust."** This is a prediction that our institutions will not be able to surmount: (1) difficulties caused by our affluence and (2) the discontent of some of our Negro citizens.

I remember similar predictions when the challenge was that of deep depression. There were many then who thought the country was doomed. They were wrong.

After World War II, there were many who forecast dire trouble for America. Andrei Vyshinsky, for example, was quite confident that we were headed for a cataclysmic depression in 1949 when the economy went into a recession. That forecast, too, was wrong.

How much nicer it is to have to worry about the crisis caused by affluence than the ones caused by depression!

In my judgment, our biggest problem is that bright young men such as you—who should be full of pride in what unfettered human beings have accomplished under a political system that pessimists 150 years ago said would never work—are even more negative than those eighteenth and nineteenth-century authoritarians who were convinced that the common man could not be entrusted with political freedom.

Instead of exhibiting enthusiasm for what has been accomplished already and determination to make our institutions work even better in the future, you talk as though we had been rushing madly toward the precipice for 200 years and were now on the verge of tumbling over. There seems to be some lack of historical perspective here.

I am confident that our institutions can adjust to changing conditions in the future as they have in the past. I hope that young people like you will prove capable of facing the future with optimism and understanding of the true nature of the challenges confronting you. This can only come from better understanding of the nature of the challenges that those who went before you met and overcame.

6. **"In the midst of . . . affluence, millions starve because Americans believe that once you have property, it is sacred—no matter that your neighbor starves and lives with rats."** I wonder if you could document the statement that millions of our people are starving. I commend to your attention an article in "U. S. News & World Report" of April 28, 1969, entitled "Truth about Hunger in America." The article reports on a study entitled "The National Nutritional Survey," directed by Dr. Arnold E. Schaefer, who is in charge of nutrition programs for the Department of Health, Education

and Welfare. "U. S. News & World Report" stated:

"In a nation of 201 million people, no outright starvation has been found." This conclusion was based on a careful study of a sample of 12,000 people—80 per cent having family incomes of less than $5,000 a year. That there is malnutrition no one would deny, but starvation is apparently very rare.

If it were true that millions were starving, I presume that it would have been a simple matter for CBS to find a child dying of starvation to portray in its now-famous documentary, "Hunger in America." Instead, it has now been proven, I understand, that CBS showed a baby dying of complications related to premature birth that had nothing to do with nutrition and falsely told its viewers that the baby was dying of starvation.

This points up one of our serious problems—the willingness of people to exaggerate and distort the facts in order to prove a point. This misinforms, misleads and creates conflict and tension, because people who have a different understanding of the facts will probably reach very different conclusions and will advocate different policies. We need much more dedication to factual accuracy to reduce tension and conflict.

I have commented in No. 3 above on the idea that Americans believe property is sacred. I would like to point out that New York City alone spends about 2 billion dollars a year, representing property taken from taxpayers, to support those who are unable to support themselves. I have traveled in many countries of the world, and I have seen no people more inclined to give to support their neighbors in need than are the Americans. This has been manifest not only in our domestic programs but in our assistance to foreign lands as well.

Since 1946, we have expended 135 billion dollars in aid to

---

*House Committee on Appropriations, Agriculture Sub-committee, Hearings on Department of Agriculture Appropriations for 1970, Part V, pp. 59-61.

foreign countries, including substantial amounts given to aid the enemies we defeated in World War II. Never before in history has a victorious power shown such generosity— demanding no reparations or tribute but giving huge amounts of aid to help the defeated survive and revive their economies.

There may be those who will tell you this was all done for ulterior motives. These are the people who seem to be unable to conceive of human beings acting for noble reasons. Perhaps this is a reflection of their own character.

7. **"American corporations exploit foreign labor and resources in Latin America."** American capital has played an important role in assisting Latin-American countries in the development of their resources and in providing employment for their people. If putting up the money to bring in machinery, build roads and pipelines, erect plants and build communications networks is exploitation, American businessmen will have to plead guilty. If hiring and training workers for higher wages than any local employer is willing to pay is exploiting labor, again our businessmen will have to plead guilty.

The simple fact is that most of the Latin-American countries have not only welcomed "exploitation" of this kind but are complaining that we are not doing enough of it today. Countries that have not benefited from such "exploitation" in recent years—such as the U.A.R. (United Arab Republic), which has been fiercely socialistic—are beginning to wonder how they can get some of it. Here is what Dr. Mohamed Abu Shady, chairman of the National Bank of Egypt—a government bank—wrote in the leading Egyptian paper, "Al Ahram," on January 15, 1969:

"There is agreement on the necessity of working to attract foreign capital, in one way or another, because there can be no real development otherwise. However, the solutions presented take only a partial view of the prob-

53

Machiz: *"American corporations exploit foreign labor and resources in Latin America."*

Robertson: *"American capital has played an important role in assisting Latin American countries in the development of their resources and in providing employment for their people."*

Photo shows Chile's Chuquicamata Open Pit Copper Mine, the largest in the world, developed by Anaconda Copper Corporation.

—COURTESY: ANACONDA COPPER CORPORATION

lem . . . because the situation, first and foremost, calls for creating a suitable atmosphere for bringing in foreign capital."

Dr. Mohamed Abu Shady is more practical than some who think that they can obtain the benefits of foreign investment in their countries without permitting returns to the investors that are attractive to them.

8. **"Human rights must be placed above both property and majority rights."** This is the nub of the debate. What you are saying is: "The majority does not agree with my values. Down with the majority. Don't waste time trying to reason and persuade. The evils are so great and so intolerable that they must be swept away by decree as fast as possible."

And so it is that tyrannies have always begun. After the abdication of the Czar, the leadership of Russia fell into the hands of the Social Democrat Kerensky, who respected democratic processes and the preservation of civil rights, including the ownership of property. That was not satisfactory to Lenin. Democracy was overthrown, and the leadership fell to a highly "righteous" minority—the Bolshevik elite.

The result has been, in the words of Djilas, the clamping down of an iron fist under which "there is room for neither air nor light." The personal right of property, which so troubles you, was abolished—with the result that every citizen became completely dependent for his livelihood on the exclusive elite who controlled all property. The sturdy yeomen known in the U.S.S.R. as "kulaks" were starved and slaughtered. Literally millions were put in slave-labor camps.

The privileges of the few abounded, the rights of the many ceased to exist. And all this was done in the name of placing human rights above property rights. That slogan has an evil sound to the oppressed people of Eastern Europe, China, North Vietnam, North Korea and Cuba. Where, they ask, are the most-elementary human rights that they used to enjoy under the regimes the Communists overthrew? At least, they say, let those of us who do not want to live under the iron fist leave.

This is all that Boris Kochubinsky, a Jewish engineer from Kiev, asked of the Soviet state: He and his wife wanted to go to Israel. They were forced out of their jobs and then arrested last November. Two weeks ago Boris Kochubinsky was sentenced to three years in prison because he and his wife dared to publicly protest the fact that they were denied permission to emigrate to Israel.

I do not know whether Lenin and his associates thought that their demand for placing human rights above property rights would ever lead to this tragic absurdity. But it has. And once you institute a system of government that gives you or anyone else the right to dictate, this is what you risk.

Sincerely yours,

J. L. Robertson

part 4

the
defenders

THE PUBLICATION OF THE EXCHANGE of letters between Marc Machiz and myself stimulated a new flood of mail. It quickly became apparent that the division of opinion was not strictly on generational lines. The great majority who wrote to me applauded and supported the position that I had defended, and most of them were clearly adults. I have included in this compilation some of these letters, partly to show the depth and range of interest in this matter, and partly because I recognized as I read the letters that there are many people in this country who are capable of making a substantive contribution to this great debate.

I was particularly pleased to find that a number of these who belong to the "under-thirty" generation had read what I had to say and reacted positively to it. Several of these letters are included, and I hope that these young people may be effective in communicating to their peers what we of the older generation have failed to communicate in many cases.

August 6, 1969

Dear Mr. Robertson:

I read the letter Marc Machiz and yourself had written. I must say, sir, I had changed my ideas on the "Older Generation," completely.

Marc had brought out some strong points in the American system that I felt should have been changed. His idea of "human rights" above "property rights" had at first made me think he was right, but when I read your reply, "We erect no Berlin Walls around the United States. There is no off-limits zone around our borders," you were right. We are not forced to stay here in this country, but the right to leave and enter is our right.

When Marc also said that we let our neighbors starve and live with rats, we do no such thing. I have lived in Milwaukee's outer city for the first seven years of my life. Things were bad for us, but I know people cared about us. We had the church there to help us, they gave us the faith to live. There was the Good Will Industry, Salvation Army, Y.M.C.A., Y.W.C.A., Boys and Girls Scouts, and later there came Welfare, Model Cities programs, money management programs, and even rat control, and even more. Adults go to school to learn a trade, to make their life better. People do care, but one has to be in need of help to find out the good quality in his fellow man. We would not let anyone starve.

When he brought out the issue of busing students, what made him mad was that people came out in record numbers to vote "No." I would be mad too, but one can't change one's feelings. It is the right of everybody to express what he feels, whether it be bad or not. What one says is his right, and his belief.

In telling of the right to own property is not absolute, you said a government has to meet expenses. I have always felt if I am good enough to pay taxes, then I am good enough to vote. But the expenses of the government don't affect me too

58

bad. It made me think of all the things I use, and see. Milwaukee is just full of beautiful parks, there are so many. Rivers in the city are being cleaned up. The expressways, street and alley lightings, policemen, firemen, postmen, public buildings such as zoos, museums, park buildings, the city fountains, and many bridges, public river and lake dockings, sewers, water mains, smog control, welfare, street cleaning, schools, cleaning of beaches and parks, and this goes on, and on. I use almost all of these things, and the little taxes I give helps the public.

Mr. Robertson, your generation will not depart from America. Your ideas and morals and lessons will not be forgotten by the future. The SDS is on the climb now, but they too will leave the scene. They are just a happening, and they will make us sick just as the Hippies are to us now. With God's help and people like you, we will make it a better world for all.

Peace be with you.
Denis M. Hansen
Milwaukee, Wisconsin

July 10, 1969

Dear Mr. Robertson:

It is timely that the more mature persons in our country take the necessary time to create thought provoking approaches to some of the problems which seem to bother so many young people today. Based on the contents of Marc Machiz's article, he apparently—like so many others—is ready to stand up and wave the flag about all the things which he considers wrong in the way the so-called establishment performs under today's conditions.

Each of us, of course, has passed the same milestones as the young people in our high schools today; and in many cases, many of us were just as concerned with conditions as they existed during our youth. Unfortunately for most of us, we have no magic formula for correcting any wrongs or persuading the majority of citizens that our own ideas would lead them to living conditions which would be ideal for all of our people.

There is a very dire need for the voice of experience to lead the young people in the United States, since they appear to be so eager to right so many things that appear so wrong to their generation. Perhaps in the next 25 years the present high school crowd will have an opportunity to assume the leadership in this country and give those of us who remain a chance to appraise the results which they have obtained in changing so many of the things to which they seem to be opposed. After reading your article, we feel that the logical minds among the youth would certainly take a broader viewpoint and assume a constructive posture, rather than a destructive approach to everything that is distasteful to them.

We hope that you will again have an opportunity to address yourself on the national level to these problems.

Yours very truly,
Louis A. Barnes
Stow, Ohio

July 2, 1969

Dear Mr. Machiz:

Your letter to Mr. Lawrence and Mr. Robertson's reply will doubtless bring you no end of mail. I venture a couple of points.

For over 30 years now I have been teaching (or trying to teach) economics here at Columbia. Not a little of research and study has gone along with my efforts. And I yield to no one in my desire to help mankind. Progress has been substantial. At least when I ask students to try to list 20 or so criteria by which a society should be judged and compare the present with 15, 25 or more years ago—well, you might try to do so. And on those which are not more advanced today (pollution, crime, manners (?), and student spelling, as a few), there are some we can see how to deal with, others not. The great one—ability to live with each other, keeping the peace—baffles us as it did the ancestors of our remotest grandparents.

My second reenforces Mr. Robertson. This year has been a sabbatical for me, and I have travelled perhaps 70,000 miles over much of the noncommunist world. What Gov. Robertson says about American business and its presence—and American values and accomplishments—conforms overwhelmingly with my impressions.

Best of good wishes. I cannot do other than plead for a decent fairness in judging the elements of strength in the record of the generation of the majority which, you feel, leaves so much to be desired.

Very truly yours,
C. Lowell Harriss
New York City, New York

July 9, 1969

Dear Governor Robertson:

I am particularly impressed by your response to the high school student with "radical" beliefs. It is not surprising that most young people are idealistic because this has been true with recent generations. Nor is it surprising that the views expressed by thoughtful young people reflect an almost complete disregard for economic security. Their only experience has been that of living in times of broad economic growth and prosperity. Accordingly, those of us who have a longer perspective in economic and allied events have a great deal of listening to do but we must try diligently, as you have done, to reason from our perspective to demonstrate why we see a great deal of merit in our current system and are not prepared to discard it for a program of idealism.

Congratulations! I hope that your remarks receive very wide readership. We are encouraging many of our people to study what you have said.

Sincerely,
Walter E. Hoadley
San Francisco, California

July 3, 1969

Dear Mr. Robertson:

In reference to your excellent and timely letter, "The Other Side," in the July 7th issue of "U. S. News and World Report."

As parents and grandparents we thank you for saying so well some of the things many of us have wanted to say, but did not have your keen analysis and the ability to express them.

There has always been a generation gap and it is well there should be one. We as adults should not expect young people to be completely satisfied with the status quo, as we advance to new things with their wonderful enthusiasm and fresh look at life.

Centuries of achievement in living together as human beings did not come about with the assumption that human rights are maximized with the suspension or curtailment of property rights. As you have said so well this is when the Hitler's come marching in.

Thank you again, for your fine letter and we appreciate men of your caliber who take the time and effort to reply to young people like Mr. Machiz. Your letter gives us a feeling of pride in America and the things America stands for. We hope he reads it carefully and understands what you're saying to all would be world shakers and those who would destroy the American system.

Our sincere best wishes to you.

Appreciatively yours,
Mr. and Mrs. D. E. Kinder
Chicago, Illinois

July 1, 1969

Dear Mr. Robertson:

For some the generation gap means a disagreement over hair length, taste in clothes, or religious beliefs. But I think what is the most disturbing part of the generation gap is the fact that so many intelligent young people are substituting emotion for reason, and are willing to turn to violence to answer the problems of America.

Though America's record for almost 200 years has been an example unequaled by any country, today more than ever we hear whispers of violence and of revolution. And at times these whispers have turned into actions and these actions have been justified by too many people.

I am a college student who does not share "radical" beliefs with certain others of my generation. I want to see a better America, and I want to help improve the lot of every American, but I know that this can never be achieved by those who would impose their beliefs of a better America upon others. I think Mr. Machiz is right when he says that "we have reached a turning point." It is a point at which many nations have found themselves at one time or another in this century. But I think the issue quickly narrows down to this—will the majority of peaceful Americans allow a violent minority, which is vociferous and energetic, to determine the future course of this country because they believe they have the answers to America's problems?

This radical minority, made up of mostly young people,

sees America as an imperialistic nation concerned with little more than making money and exploiting its power and wealth around the world. They hold a distorted picture of the history of America and they are cynical and suspicious of every move America has made or is making. They see what they believe to be American injustices but they fail to comprehend the truth about Czechoslovakia, Estonia, Latvia, Lithuania, Tibet, and all the other captive nations of the world. They believe Americans are prisoners in an evil system, yet they know little of the Berlin Wall or the Iron Curtain. They frown upon our concept of freedom, yet they can't explain why against tremendous odds, and in the face of almost certain failure, people of East Berlin risk and lose their lives in the hope of escaping to West Berlin.

They have little confidence in America's institutions which they claim are outdated, corrupt, and too slow moving to deal successfully with America's problems. Yet history has shown that these same institutions have outlived and survived every crisis America has had to face in the last two centuries including total war, immense hunger and unemployment, and violent racial conflict.

And what I believe is so dangerous about all this, is that this minority believes it can put itself above the law, and that it can choose for itself what to obey and what not to obey. This idea is not original. It is the very foundation of totalitarianism in this century. Mussolini and Hitler both claimed they were always right and therefore above the law—all the majority had to do was to follow and their problems would be solved. This is not what I want American government to be. John Locke said:

"And thus every man, by consenting with others to make one body politic under one government, puts himself under an obligation to everyone of that society to submit to the determination of the majority, and to be concluded by it; or else this original compact, whereby he with others incorporates into one society, would signify nothing. . . ."

This is the only path America can take if it wants to keep both democratic rule and internal order.

And thus, Mr. Robertson, I want to commend you for an exceptionally perceptive and thoughtful reply to the letter by Mr. Machiz. To those who are intent on nothing more than destroying America your words will mean little. But I know that for the much larger group of protesters, who are genuinely concerned about improving America, your words will not easily be forgotten or ignored. If more people like yourself would take the time to honestly answer some of the questions and complaints of the younger generation I know that the generation gap would quickly become narrower.

Sincerely yours,

Louis S. Rulli

Willingboro, New Jersey

July 2, 1969

Dear Mr. Robertson:

I have just finished reading your reply to Mr. Marc Machiz, and I wish to compliment you on a most objective and illuminating rebuttal.

Your defense is particularly illuminating by virtue of a key phrase. Your statement in item five . . . "there seems to be some lack of historical perspective . . ." I feel is getting very close to one of the key problem areas of our youthful "radicals."

Your own defense is bolstered by a keen awareness of the social and political evolutions that have produced our system of government. Naturally, your maturity and experience contribute to this awareness and yet I venture to say that your formal education, as well as your home environment as a young man, strongly contributed to your historical perspective. Unfortunately, it appears that our young "radicals" or "liberals" are ignorant in this respect both by virtue of omission and commission. A review of their philosophies and objectives reveals both a distorted analysis of history and a selective rejection of those precepts which would expose fallacies in their ideas.

We bear an awesome responsibility with regard to this lack of perception in that many of us fail to profess sufficient respect for our national evolution to impart a proper perspective to our children and to demand that our schools and universities teach and stimulate an understanding and appreciation for the interaction of varied political and social theories which produced our form of government. Therefore, in my opinion, your comments have a more urgent message for parents, teachers and national leaders than Mr. Machiz and his compatriots.

Very respectfully,
W. F. Robey, Jr.
Charleston, South Carolina

July 17, 1969

Dear Mr. Robertson:

As an English-born naturalized citizen somehow it has been my privilege during many July 4th or November 11th observances in the place where I work (Unity School of Christianity) to conduct the service, speak of some facet of the Declaration of Independence or of the Constitution, then have the pledge to the flag. Just before the meeting I conducted July 2nd for Unity School (did a similar one on July 4th for our summer training school) one of my employees in the Department handed to me the "U. S. News and World Report" of July 7th. I was so deeply touched with your letter (and also the one from the young boy) that I asked to read the entire text of your speech given May 22nd in Omaha, Nebraska. I have read it over and over and over; I have read it aloud to friends and relatives. It almost seems that the words **you** have written are **my** words—at least they are my sentiments and couched in far better words than I could write.

This is now my country; I became naturalized with full realization of what I was doing. I had married an American citizen, and I intended to take the best this country had to offer and I felt it was entitled to the best I could offer in return. Because of this I feel so deeply all the things you brought out in your talk, and I have never hesitated when asked to take something patriotic—I feel it is one way I can say to America, "Thank you, my adopted country."

I can't help thinking that if the young boy to whom your reply was given is really thinking deeply—and his letter would so indicate—he will get the deep inner meaning of your letter. Bless you for being an American citizen—a "concerned citizen"—who is not afraid to speak up and not afraid to say that there **is** something good in what went before us.

Bless you and may God's smile be upon all your undertakings.

Yours very sincerely,
Vera Dawson Tait
Lee's Summit, Missouri

August 6, 1969

Dear Governor Robertson:

Since your published articles and Marc's letter are sincere expressions of each of your convictions, they warrant an equally reflective and straightforward reply.

As an individual whose life has been dominated and influenced by the "conservative" Midwest, and as a young lawyer, a profession which identifies me as a member of the "establishment," my beliefs do, not surprisingly, more closely correspond with those in your articles than with Marc's "radical" beliefs. Consequently, unlike Marc, I do not believe that America's "institutions do not merit support." Rather, in my judgment, America's institutions and the values on which they were founded and operate not only deserve but command each individual's efforts to preserve and perpetuate them.

Why should we support and continue our institutions? To begin with, your June 9 article clearly presented the moral values, respect for truth, respect for human dignity, consideration for the rights of others, and the operational values of majority rule and majority respect for the rights of the minority. They are worthy of preservation and perpetuation for the reason that they have historically proven themselves. These values have formed, I believe, the foundation on which our institutions were established and in conjunction with which they grew and prospered. In turn, these institutions have proven historically to be the providers of economic well-being and of personal rights and freedom for a number of people greater than has seldom ever before been achieved. Since our institutions have historically achieved this, they have proven, I believe, that if we are willing to labor to make them succeed, the institutions are capable of bringing equal rights and opportunities to all Americans whether Negro, Indian, or Mexican-American as well as economic well-being to the poor.

Secondly, the reasons frequently stated and examples cited by Marc and others do not convince me that our American institutions have not and will not function in such a manner so as to deserve our support rather than our resistance. Your July 7 comments adequately reply (so that it is superfluous for me to elaborate other than to cite them) to Marc's statements made in support of his contention that "America today is fundamentally on the wrong course" and that as a result "its institutions do not merit support."

Thirdly, I do not believe that actively resisting the functioning of America's institutions, whether the resistance manifests itself as unconstitutional nonviolent disobedience or as violence, will ultimately be as effective as working within the law and the institutions of our society. In his praiseworthy booklet, Concerning Dissent and Civil Disobedience, former Associate Justice of the Supreme Court, Abe Fortas, discusses the methods of attaining changes within the institutions and traditions of our society. When analyzing the Negroes' use of active resistance to achieve their fundamental rights and equal opportunities, Justice Fortas discredits violence. He convincingly explains why he is persuaded that violence is not a productive technique for accomplishing the objectives of the Negroes. He, in fact, concludes:

"Violence is never defensible—and it has never succeeded in securing massive reform in an open society where there were **alternative methods of winning the minds of others to one's cause and securing changes in the government or its policies.**"

Alternatives to violence through which change can be accomplished within the law, institutions and traditions of our society are available to both the Negro and to the rebellious youth. They are the guarantees of speech, press and peaceable assembly of the First Amendment and active participation in the political processes including the political parties and the ballot box.

In a preceding paragraph, I praised our present institutions and the values on which they were founded for the liberty and justice and economic well-being that they have brought to a vast number of people. Nonetheless, we are all aware of our society's deficiencies. As we have read frequently, and as an American educator Robert Hutchins states dramatically:

69

"Our industrial expansion brought us wealth, more abundant goods and pollution. Mass transportation will get us almost anywhere, except to the woods, fields and streams we've had to destroy to build highways. Our cities today have everything—giant business complexes, indoor shopping centers, symphonies and rats."

Indeed our nation presently is beset with almost every problem, including poverty, minority groups which are denied their fundamental rights and equal opportunities, rapidly increasing crime, and destructive riots to enumerate only a few. Everything could be better.

How to make our institutions work to solve these problems should be a constant drum-roll in our contemplations of the problems of our society. Our basic requirement is the presence of individuals who are willing to contribute diligence, new solutions, and concerned intelligent leadership. Your article is one more impetus motivating individuals from merely an awareness of the problems, into activity producing the enlightened leadership that our institutions demand if the values on which they are founded are to be preserved and perpetuated. As man's landing on the moon demonstrates, another requirement for making our institutions work to solve a problem is the sufficient dedication of time and money. Let us re-examine the allocation of our resources and channel them as soon as possible from space and the war in Vietnam into solving the multitude of domestic problems. For example, let us review the priorities of the federal government which, as Secretary of Housing and Urban Development George Romney pointed out at the Western States Governor's Conference in Seattle on July 28, we spent 24 billion on the Apollo program while our ghettos remain unfit for human beings, our cities decay, our environment becomes covered with litter and cement, and our air and water become polluted.

While working to solve the problems facing our society, we also must deal with the rebellious students, convincing them that it is better to work within the laws, institutions, and traditions of our society than to oppose them. Education is, I believe, a partial answer. An interview with Professor Sidney Hook, in the May 19, 1969, issue of "U. S. News and World Report" quoted him as saying the following:

"The truth is that the students are completely unhistorical. They have no perspective upon events. They do not compare the situation today with what it was like in the past. They expect overnight transformations which in the nature of the case can't take place if one understands history and the elements of human psychology."

In my judgment, if the rebellious students are to be persuaded to work within our institutions to obtain change, education must impart a sense of historical perspective, a sense of reality about the time and effort that is required to achieve fundamental social change, and an awareness of the progress that has been and is being made. In addition, I am convinced that nothing will succeed to quell the rebellious students and create in them a willingness to support and work within our institutions as the successful removal of the political, social, and economic inequities in our society and the quick progress toward that end. We should, I believe, redouble our efforts to attain the rights and opportunities to which the Negro and other minority groups are entitled, to bring economic well-being to the poor, and to do something about the other worth-while grievances of the students.

In the meantime, I believe that our society should not tolerate the violation of a law by an individual or a group solely as a technique of demonstration when alternative methods of protest are available. Certainly protest and criticism with demonstration, organization and assembly within the limits of the Constitution must be allowed and en-

71

couraged. However demonstration beyond the limits of the law, which causes the destruction of property and deprives or interferes with the rights of others, cannot be permitted if an organized society is to survive.

As an alternative to tolerating violation of the law, society can punish the offenders. Since many of the rebellious youth are convinced that their cause is righteous, they do not seem to easily accept the fact that the law and the punishment prescribed for its violation applies to them both on and off campus. As a result, the mechanical application of the punishment the law prescribes will, I fear, only cause further disillusionment with a society and its institutions that they already reject. Abe Fortas, in his booklet Concerning Dissent and Civil Disobedience sees the dilemma of punishing the youth clearly and is worth if I may, extensively quoting:

". . . (P)erhaps it is a beginning to separate student activities which are nonviolent from those which involve assault or damage to persons or property. Where the law violation is nonviolent or technical (such as blocking entrance to a campus building, or even orderly occupancy of a university facility), there may be sense in patient forbearance despite the wrong that the action involves. But violent activities, in my judgment, should be regarded and treated as intolerable. Punishment of on-campus violence involves risks. Particularly in respect to the youth-generation, it should be undertaken only after all efforts to persuade, patiently applied, have been exhausted. But the toleration of violence involves, I think, even greater risks, not only of present damage and injury but of erosion of the base of an ordered society. The point, I think, is not whether the aggressor should be halted and punished, but how; and it is here that moderation, consideration, and sympathetic understanding should play their part."

The foregoing paragraphs, which include some thoughts that your two articles evoked, admittedly contain no new solutions to the problems discussed, but do stand as my sincere beliefs and as a step in the process of thinking the problems through in the hope of arriving at a worthwhile contribution to the laws and institutions of our society.

Respectively yours,
William E. Zwink
Loup City, Nebraska

Chief Justice Warren E. Burger, in an address at Ripon College, Ripon, Wisconsin, May 21, 1967, evidenced an awareness that how a person is punished is just as important as the determination of his guilt. Too often, said Justice Burger, once the issue of guilt is decided, we treat the convicted as "rubbish," and incarcerate him in a prison that will do little if anything to ensure that he will be a better person when he returns to society. I am convinced, as Justice Burger seems to be, that punishment for violation of the law must be a constructive process not only for the convicted of all ages, but especially for the youthful offender, and that if the dilemma of how society punishes the rebellious youth is not tackled, society will punish only the flagrant violators. It may ignore massive numbers of violators because it is either not equipped to efficiently cope with such numbers or realizes that imprisonment may only leave the youth a poorer person and that in an increasingly affluent society, the power of a monetary fine is impaired. Society must therefore labor with the problem of how we punish the offender just as diligently, inventively, and urgently as with the problems of the economic welfare of the poor and the denial of the rights and opportunities of the minorities. Otherwise the violators of the law may not be constructively punished, which must be done to preserve an organized democratic society as we know it.

part 5

the critics: philosophy and institutions

THE PUBLICATION OF THE CORRESPONDENCE with Marc Machiz has stimulated a number of people who sympathized with his views to write to me. Not all of these were young, but the majority were. Their letters gave me a broader view of the ideas and thinking of our troubled younger generation.

I felt about them as I had about Marc. They deserved to have answers to the questions they raised. Since they had taken the trouble to write to me, sometimes at considerable length and with great feeling, I felt that I had the responsibility of giving them the best answers I could.

As the letters came in and the replies went out, I found myself more and more intrigued by this unusual dialogue. It was enlightening to me to learn what was troubling these articulate young people, and I hope that a few of them, at least, may have profited from my efforts to show them a side of the coin that they may have overlooked.

I had had many letters from people who expressed the hope that the exchange with Marc Machiz might be read by all the youth of the country. Friends of mine who saw the ensuing correspondence urged that these letters also be published so that they might have a wider readership. As I reflected on the matter, I came to feel that publication might be helpful in bringing about a better understanding between the generations.

Had the letters, both the incoming and the outgoing, been written with publication in mind, I am sure they would have been more polished and some of the points might have been more carefully argued. On the other hand, the letters as written had the virtue of being an honest reflection of the way many people were thinking in mid-1969. If there were a lack of polish and a tendency towards emotional overstatement, there was also a feeling that the writers were flesh and blood human beings stating what they honestly believed.

The letters in this section are, I think, an honest reflection of the feelings of many concerned Americans who are—for one reason or another—critical of some aspects of our basic philosophy and our institutions.

A section that follows is devoted to letters that were concerned with narrower issues. In neither section are all of the problems confronting us covered, but the selection has been determined by my correspondents, not by me. I have tried to include all of the critical letters that were not of the "crank" variety or did not essentially duplicate points made better by others.

Any feeling of impatience at the lengthy discussion of the issues included in these letters is understandable. Those of us who have reached our maturity have long since found our basic philosophy. We may not realize or appreciate that many of our young people are groping for the answers to questions that we have forgotten even existed. This is the generation gap that we have to try to bridge. We must strive for agreement on the basic philosophical issues. There are many things we can and should disagree about. It would be profoundly distressing if we ever found ourselves all thinking exactly alike on all questions. But we cannot successfully function as a nation if the overwhelming majority cannot agree on fundamental principles.

One of the letters I received in July 1969 was from a very articulate young lady in the mid-west who did not wish her letter to be published in this volume. Because the points she raised had seemed to me to merit the fairly detailed reply which I sent her, I thought it fitting that they be summarized and my reply be included here. The following is, I think, a fair summary of her major points.

1. The economic and political system in the United States is not consistent with the ideals embodied in the Declaration of Independence and the Constitution. While the average man is idealistic and aspires to a world free of tyranny where ordinary people can live in peace and harmony, there are a lot of things that are incongruent in the so-called "establishment." The federal government, for example, pays out large sums of money to industry for research and development, but these grants are really "unworthy subsidies." She quotes the following from a column by Drew Pearson and Jack Anderson to demonstrate this point:

"For instance, General Electric, a company which has been convicted of wanton criminal violation of the antitrust act, and fined over a million dollars, with prison, nevertheless received $356,079,000 for alleged research and development in the last year figures were available, namely, 1966."

"Harvey Aluminum, a company which last year received a tax forgiveness bonanza of $2 million, thanks to a last-minute amendment hung on the so-called Christmas Tree bill, by Sen. Vance Hartke, D-Ind., got a nice present from Uncle Sam to the tune of $1,138,000 for alleged research and development. This is a company without many technical skills except when it comes to lobbying and politics. Carmen Warschaw, the sister of its top partner, has long been democratic chairman of Southern California."

2. The rich are favored and the poor are discriminated against in

our tax system. To support this, she submitted the following quotations:

a. *"Surpringly, it's the poor, not the rich, who pay the bigger share of earnings in taxes. A new study shows why there's a flurry of tax plans to help the poor."*

b. *". . . true enough, the large-propertied elements in the United States see to it that they are very lightly taxed—many with $5 million or more of steady income often paying no tax at all for many years while a man with a miserable $2,000 income, perhaps after years of no income, denies his family medical or dental care in order to pay tax!"*

3. The Declaration of Independence, in stating that all men are endowed with certain inalienable rights, among them life, liberty and the pursuit of happiness, should be interpreted to mean that everyone should be entitled to medical care regardless of ability to pay. This should also be true of higher education, but the fact is that everyone cannot get all the medical attention they need or all the education they want in this country.

4. It is not proper to say that an American is free to leave his country at any time he chooses. For one thing, you need to have the price of a ticket and the know-how to obtain a passport. But people who are critical of many conditions that prevail here also love the country and its ideals. They do not want to leave; they merely want to make the country a better place in which to live.

5. While it is true that our institutions can adjust to changing needs, it appears that needed adjustments have sometimes come about only because of riots or civil disobedience. Thus the auto makers in Detroit found it advisable to hire 20,000 hard core unemployed after the riots there, but not before. The blacks are making progress today, but nothing is being done for the Mexicans and Indians who are not rioting.

6. Our economic aid to Europe after World War II was generous, but it was not given solely for altruistic reasons, and if it was altruism that got us into Vietnam, then it was misplaced.

7. It is an error to compare communistic dictatorships with

capitalistic democracies, and thus equate communism with dictatorship and capitalism with democracy. Pure capitalism is at least as evil as communism, as the experience with the so-called "Robber Barons" in the United States in the latter part of the 19th century shows. The most equitable system lies between capitalism and communism.

8. The United States is not perfect and probably never will be, but perfection is what we must strive for.

I replied as follows:

Dear XXXXXXXXXX:

It was nice of you to take the time to write to me at such length. I would like to make a few comments on the points you make.

1. It is certainly true that several years ago officials of General Electric and some other large manufacturers of electrical equipment were convicted of conspiring to violate the antitrust laws. They were indicted, tried and punished. I hardly think that you would suggest that because of this violation of law the government should never again do business with General Electric or make any use of its products or services. General Electric is one of our largest manufacturing firms and has research facilities that have been responsible for many important technological advances. I know nothing about the contracts the government has given this firm for research and development, but unless it is demonstrated otherwise I will presume that GE delivered the services it was paid for. To imply that there was something dishonorable about the transaction because many years ago certain GE officials engaged in dishonorable and illegal actions does not strike me as being either very logical or very honorable. This comment would appear to apply equally to the Harvey Aluminum contract for research and development.

I have been around Washington long enough to know that corruption, profiteering and waste do exist. However, at no time in my memory has corruption been regarded as so rampant and pervasive that its discovery would not qualify as important news. We do not find it to be the rule rather than the exception, nor do we condone it. I do not condemn the entire younger generation because there are a number of bad apples among them. Nor would I condemn the entire "establishment" because it may include some individuals of questionable ethics.

2. The statement you quoted from "U.S. News and World Report" about the tax burden impinging more heavily on low than on high income groups does not square with the findings of a study made by the Tax Foundation and published in January 1967 under the title, "Tax Burdens and Benefits of Government Expenditures by Income Class, 1961 and 1965." This study indicated that in both 1961 and 1965 the lowest income group, with income of less than $3,000, paid about 27 per cent of income in taxes of all kinds. Families with incomes in excess of $15,000 paid about 44 per cent in taxes in both years. I do not know what accounts for the discrepancy. Perhaps different time periods were included or different assumptions were made about the data that had to be estimated. It should be noted, of course, that these figures include all taxes, not simply federal income taxes which bear much more heavily on the upper income groups than they do upon the lower.

The Tax Foundation study also attempted to discover how the benefits of government expenditures were allocated. This obviously involves making a number of assumptions and generalizations, but for whatever it is worth, they concluded that families with incomes in the range of $2,000 to $3,000 in 1965 obtained benefits from government expenditures equal to 65 per cent of their incomes, while families with incomes of $15,000 and up received benefits equal to only 16 per cent of their incomes.

If this is approximately correct, it suggests that the lowest income group is getting back more than $2 in value for every dollar paid in taxes, while the income group above $15,000 is getting about 37 cents in services for each dollar paid.

Opinions may vary widely on what is equitable, but we have an additional problem in democracy. What you and I may consider equitable may not be so considered by a majority of the voters or legislators. Our tax legislation is not a model of perfection. It represents a lot of compromises, and some of these are based not on ideal conceptions of distributive justice. Perhaps that is one of the prices we pay for democracy. Of course, in drawing up tax plans, there are other things that have to be borne in mind besides the equity of the incidence of the tax on various income groups. Taxes may also serve as an incentive or disincentive for various activities—such as the consumption of alcohol or cigarettes, or the purchase of new equipment by manufacturers.

3. It would be nice if we lived in a world where everyone could have every material good and service he wanted by merely snapping his fingers, but Aladdin's lamp has long since been lost. Most goods and services cannot be supplied in the quantities that would be demanded if no price were placed upon them. Free market prices constitute a kind of rationing system that avoids compulsion and permits individuals to decide how they will allocate their limited incomes to derive the maximum personal satisfaction. This has been replaced in a number of cases by having the government either control prices or provide certain services free or at less than cost. You would like this to be done for certain services not now covered. Very likely in time your aspirations will be realized, but at the moment too many people do not agree with your judgment that this is desirable. Again, the rules of the game require that we work within the framework of persuasion to secure the desired legislative changes. Again this is a price we pay for democracy.

4. I am glad that you love America and think so well of it

that you want to stay here to work and improve it. That is the way it should be. However, the right to leave is also a precious right that is denied to the residents in the totalitarian countries. I would not suggest that our young dissidents leave **en masse,** but I did want to emphasize the fact that they have the right to do so if they wish.

5. While violence and violations of law have indeed helped some Negroes achieve benefits that they might not otherwise have obtained so quickly, the price that we have paid seems to be one of escalating violence and increasing racial tension. What the long-run costs will be remains to be seen. There are other ways of obtaining recognition of one's rights which do not leave dangerous open wounds. I am reminded that the Japanese-Americans were discriminated against to the point where a very substantial percentage of them were plucked from their homes and relocated in rather unpleasant camps during World War II. They had to overcome not only racial prejudice but also the stigma of being immigrants or descended from immigrants from a country with which we had fought a most bitter war. Their attitude was that they would try to win acceptance by being better citizens than anyone else. By and large they seem to have succeeded. I do indeed suggest working within the system. It may take both time and money, but I prefer that to blood and tyranny.

6. Your comment on our motives in giving aid to Europe in the postwar period overlooks the fact that even the USSR could have been included within the Marshall Plan if it had wished. Czechoslovakia at first accepted and then had to reverse itself on Moscow's insistence.

I am sure there is no point in discussing the motives or merits of our intervention in Vietnam with you, but I would not want you to think that I agreed with your statement that our altruism was misplaced. I see no misplaced altruism in an effort to save an entire country from the kind of bloodbath that the Communists inflicted upon Hue in February 1968 when they temporarily occupied that city. They demonstrated again that they had not changed in the least from the days when they inflicted similar massacres upon the unfortunate Vietnamese who lived north of the 17th parallel when they finally won uncontested power in that area. I am always amazed at the tendency of some of our young people to exhibit heartfelt outrage at the comparatively minor injustices that they note in our own society and at the same time accept as great heroes and humanitarians those who have brutally butchered and tortured from thousands to millions of their unfortunate, helpless subjects. But I am sure that you are not one of these.

7. You imply that we ought not to equate capitalism with democracy and communism with dictatorship. I agree in part. It is possible to have a free market private enterprise system without democracy, and it is possible to have democracy with a very much modified free market system. It is possible to have a dictatorship without communism, but there is no evidence that suggests that it is possible to have communism without a dictatorship. Communism as we know it in practice involves not only political dictatorship, but totalitarian control over virtually all social and economic activity as well. Being totally oppressive, it must deny the right of exit, thus converting entire countries into large prison camps. I find it strange that anyone would suggest that this type of political and economic organization is no worse than what America had in the 19th century, a period when millions of Europeans left countries ruled by only mildly authoritarian regimes to flock to our shores.

Actually, it is a mistake to talk about capitalism and communism as though they were true opposites. Communism in practice is far more than a system of economic organization. It is a system of total organization of society and it should be contrasted with liberalism, in both political and economic organizations. The opposite of a liberal economic system free of governmental controls is not communism, but what has been called **dirigisme.** This is a system in which the economy is rigidly controlled by the government, regardless of whether through ownership or other means. I believe that it would be correct to say that most modern economists favor something in between a completely **laissez faire** and a complete **dirigiste** economy, but the preferences I am sure are much more on the side of introducing some controls in the free economy than on the side of a completely controlled economy modified by a little freedom.

Let me conclude by saying that I am glad you are an idealist and want to work to make our country a better place. I hope you will not become discouraged when we fail to achieve that unattainable goal of perfection. The older generation tends to be much more reconciled to living in an imperfect world. We need the prodding of youthful idealists to keep us progressing, but we hope that in their haste and eagerness they do not push us over a precipice.

Sincerely,

J. L. Robertson

The following letter was originally addressed to *U. S. News and World Report,* but the addressee was stricken and the letter sent directly to me by its writer with a cover letter.

July 21, 1969

Dear Sir:

I read with a great deal of interest "One Generation Speaks to Another." Since I am closer to thirty than to 20, I am on the verge of being mistrusted; but then the liberals and the radicals of these United States are not all under 30; nevertheless Marc Machiz spoke very well as Mr. Robertson pointed out.

My purpose is to raise further issues with Mr. Robertson, and to imply, I think, that the ideas of our founding fathers have been totally sidestepped by the plutocrats—we were warned against them by Lincoln—and indeed our society is highly materialistic.

For example the other day a friend of mine asked if I ever read anything for pleasure; all I seem to have time to read is for either what I teach in the classroom or for my night-school classes. And he is correct; there is a kind of "protestant ethic" in this country that makes us feel guilty to do something for pleasure. A man who is a ballet dancer instead of an automobile mechanic is not quite right, and certainly not masculine. Rather he should live in suburbia, be interested in baseball, finances, and all of the things that make a fine American! That includes owning a copy of King James version of the Bible and having a display of his Boy Scout merit badges, especially the one that says for God and Country. Earn your way to heaven saith the great Protestant Reformers (that excludes Luther and Cramner by the way), and made for the very sectarianism that made the 19th Century revival hymns (and the brilliant satire of Mark Twain). I am certainly not a Marxist—read very little of him as a matter of fact—but I am also very much against this guilt that is imbedded into the American child, especially the male, that he must do something practical, make a good living, and own his own property, and be a proud family man.

I like the freedom I enjoy in the United States, and I am thankful for it; I further suspect that without the kinds of public education we provide I would never have gotten where I am—30 hrs. beyond the M.A. and an instructor in a small college. But I further say that we are now forcing our children into college where most of them do not belong for the sole purpose of making a good living. The college degree is too often a requirement for a good-salaried position. It is doubtful if that degree is needed; I wonder if the draft and the four years of college are not just an effort to keep the large number of people off the job-market for 4 to 6 years (and therefore prolonging "youth") (?)

The analogy—or parable—for No. 3 is good; but let's play with that idea a little more. Let's simply say that a man can only earn so much, own so much, and prices can only be so high. I do not like incentives; I do not like competition. When I am given a job to do, I do the best I can. I cannot even tell you what my salary is, but it is something barely over $8,000. Salary raises are nice, but I am not going to work any harder if they come, and I do not think that I really deserve the money I get. Considering what the grandparents that raised me made, that is more money than I ever saw before. And the presents I was given as a child were books, not toy guns, or really toys of any kind. I had my B.A. before I learned to drive.

Now the people's park in California is silly, and I suspect that most of those concerned thought so too. But there are a lot of conservatives running around yelling Communist and un-American just because someone has a beard or bell-bottoms and the youth are determined to tantalize such people and their bodyguards—the so-called Nazi pigs—just as the gods viciously teased and made "tantalize." (Have a Bullfinch around?)

Now No. 6 probably referred to the world, not just the good old U.S.A. I am not sure just how much we should give away in foreign aid, but I am sure of a moral duty that the rich should NOT get richer. If we can find a job for every man, fine, then give him a job and do not let him loaf. But I doubt there is a job for every man, and I am quite sure that we must become a welfare state with a guaranteed income and price ceiling to match. The surplus of that I rather think should be given to other peoples—but maybe that is too idealistic.

From the time I was old enough to listen to adults, I knew that the two great evils of the world were big business and politics. As I grasp for age 30 and step out of the last stages of youth, I have found little proof those who were around me as a child were wrong.

There No. 7 is a truism; I do not doubt Mr. Robertson either. But I suggest that the industrialists there are much more interested in their own pockets than the welfare of the given country, be it in Latin America, Africa, Asia, or elsewhere. I also suggest that the local governments are not much interested in the peasants either. So let me draw an analogy you can shoot holes through; the radical youth may be compared with the Abolitionists of the 1840s and 1850s and the businessman to Simon Legree (unfortunate that she selected the name Simon, isn't it?).

And finally No. 8. Have you not side-stepped the real issue here? Pulling a comparison out of Russia is beside the point; it smacks of a John Birchite subtly suggesting subversion, or at best, look how much better off we are than the people in Russia.

We are not comparing the U.S. to any other country past or present. We are comparing it to the idealism of our forefathers and saying that in that comparison and that comparison only we have failed! Do not hand me what someone else is doing, that is a teenager saying that he wants speckled pants because his buddy has a pair, or the housewife trying to keep ahead of the Jones.

It is obvious we are finer than other countries in the world. But why are we not better? Better than we are now?

It all boils down to why are people not nicer, kinder, and more thoughtful than they are? Freedom of religion and a finer, greater education do not seem to be the answer if the U.S.A. experiment is the result of that experiment.

I do not have long hair; I am not a member of the great unwashed; but I am not a banker either, and I have no intention of becoming either one!

Regards,
Robert R. Lawrence
Louisville, Kentucky

August 11, 1969

Dear Mr. Lawrence:

Thank you for adding another interesting letter to the many I have received concerning the letter to Marc Machiz. One of the things that impresses me most about the critical correspondence such as yours is the tendency of the writers to make statements that they themselves would probably recognize as too sweeping or as factually unsupportable if they would only take the trouble to examine them critically.

I am amazed that anyone would seriously assert that Americans "feel guilty to do something for pleasure." If that were true, we would certainly be a highly guilt-ridden people, because the amount of time and money that we devote to recreational activities is enormous. For example, in 1968 Americans spent about $34 billion for recreational activities and equipment. We spent nearly $10 billion on tobacco products and about $15 billion on alcoholic beverages. Foreign travel, much of it for recreational purposes, came to more than $4 billion. These expenditures accounted for nearly 12 per cent of our total expenditures for personal consumption in 1968. They do not include many expenditures that were largely pleasure-oriented, such as buying new automobiles when the old one was still quite serviceable and buying food, clothing and household furnishings which in quantity and quality was in excess of the minimum required to meet our needs. I am sure that many people feel that a good case could be made that we as people spend too much time and money on frivolous things.

On the other hand, I would not take issue with your statement that most American children grow up to aspire to do something practical, make a good living, own property and rear good families. I do not think that that is a peculiar characteristic of Americans, however. It seems to be rather widespread in the world. This perhaps explains why the human race has survived and attained its present level of civilization. It seems to be a law of nature that every species develops its distinctive pattern of behavior. Some patterns have been more successful than others. In the human species there has been considerable diversity, but those subgroupings that have tended toward indolence and weak parental concern for the welfare of the children have not thrived as well as those that have been more industrious and family centered. This is especially true where these subgroups have been in competition with each other. You may personally prefer a society that does not look down on indolence, but you should recognize that even the indolent in our society would be far more miserable than they are if most of us were not by nature industrious. They should therefore be grateful for the industry of the majority. It would be to their great disadvantage if you were successful in persuading everyone that they should not work, save and rear good families.

Another characteristic that I have noted in some of the letters that I have received is the tendency to assume that human nature is either not what it actually is or that it could be easily changed. Like it or not, the acquisitive instinct is deeply imbedded in man. It has generally been found that most people will work better when they are offered material incentives than when they are coerced. There are many cases where people will extend themselves for altruistic motives—such as searching for a lost child—but it has been found that this does not suffice for activities that require work over an indefinite period of time. Nearly everyone who has reflected on this characteristic of the human and upon what appear to be general economic laws agrees that we get more rational economic allocation of resources under a system which permits prices and wages to fluctuate more or less freely in response to the forces of supply and demand. The reason for this is that we have an enormous number of diverse economic transactions that are taking place every hour of the day. They interact in highly complex ways, and no single human mind even with the aid of the best computers is able to keep pace with changes in relationships that constantly occur. Experience both in this country and in other lands that have tried centralized control of prices and wages strongly indicates that these controls very quickly produce great injustices and irrationalities. The individual worker, consumer, merchant, manufacturer, etc., tends to respond in ways that will maximize his own material advantage, and when the controls are applied this frequently produces results that the controllers neither expected nor wanted.

Many people are dissatisfied with the allocation of resources that results under free market conditions, but the practical alternative is not some imaginary perfect allocation, but what we know happens under the alternatives available to us. We and others have experimented with these and have found them to be even less satisfactory as a general rule.

Your suggestion that we ought not to draw comparisons with other countries but only with some ideal system of government overlooks the fact that in our desire to improve our situation we have an obligation to make sure that we do not make it worse. It is not only legitimate but essential that we study the results of experiments with other systems that have actually been tried. This is especially valid in cases where those systems were inaugurated with the promise that they would achieve a close approximation of the ideal society. It is easy to dream and easy to promise. But we must not be so gullible as to accept dreams and promises which actual experience has shown to be empty and whose consequences have been tragic.

Sincerely,

J. L. Robertson

Mr. Lawrence favored me with a thoughtful reply to the above letter, pointing out that I had misunderstood his point about Americans feeling guilty to do things for pleasure. The following excerpts give the essence of his comment:

"When I speak of Americans feeling 'guilty to do something for pleasure,' I meant only in the area of the arts! I frankly do not consider fishing, camping, tobacco, new automobiles, and so forth as even arguable. Part of this is the average citizens' only outlet for 'time off' and the latter is part of the materialism that is part of the American philosophy (dating according to D. H. Lawrence from Franklin's Autobiography). I suspect as a people we do 'spend too much time and money on frivolous things,' but my point concerned only the concept of classical music, poetry, opera, ballet, etc. This is usually termed a waste of time, impractical. It is this—the attitude toward the poet, the artist, that I was making my polemic. You also mentioned foreign travel among the pleasures we Americans enjoy. There I am not so sure. The only people that I know who are interested in going abroad are those who have a real interest in making studies of art, architecture, and for personal or scholarly purposes, to visit authors' residences and libraries. Here my knowledge is even more limited.

"Further you suggest that there is nothing wrong with having children brought up to 'aspire to do something practical, make a good living, own property, and rear good families' as it would seem to be the basis for the survival of the human race, and the reason that it has 'attained its present level of civilization.' That may be true, but I am not especially happy with that present level, because there is more hate than kindness surrounding us.

"I was not thinking of indolence, as a way of being, in the sense of a 'do-nothing' person surviving on welfare. That is obviously a very complex problem, especially in our urban society. Just as an aside, President Nixon's speech on that subject was the first time I felt he said something, and it also was, to my mind, a logical and hopefully workable system. Generally speaking, I fear we are moving toward the Roman dole.

"I like industrious people, and prefer only to associate with them. But I also like to think that industriousness comes from within, not from an incentive. If I were promised an A in every course I took, I really doubt I would work less hard; I am in the class room to learn, not to earn a grade. I do not like people who just work to earn, to better themselves materialistically. Yet, I do think that that is the American way. I do use property as a kind of metaphor for the absolute avarice that is a god to the American way of being. It was our Puritan forefathers, not the landed gentry of the South, that it seems to me gave us the great philosophy to build industry and to pioneer-west. There is something just plain repulsive about a businessman, to me. You explain it this way: 'The individual worker, consumer, merchant, manufacturer, etc., tends to respond in ways that will maximize his own material advantage, and when the controls are applied this frequently produces results that the controllers neither expected nor wanted.' Why would one be more interested in himself and in his family than in the general good society? As long as the human race moves on incentive—I wonder if that is not synonymous with greed?—then I am not proud to be a member of the human race.

"You speak of practical alternatives to this 'allocation of resources'—which I take to mean wages and profits—; one like myself cannot think in terms of practical alternatives. I think in terms of gentleness, kindness, and love. These are impractical on any level but the most personal, yet I do not understand why.

"You end your letter this way: 'It is easy to dream and easy to promise. But we must not be so gullible as to accept dreams and promises which actual experience has shown to be empty and whose consequences have been tragic.'

"The tragic answer to this comment of yours, for our century anyway, was given back in the 20's by the Lost Generation. They ranged from the frantic life of Hemingway's Jake Barnes to those several famous works of T. S. Eliot's, 'The Love Song of J. Alfred Profrock' (ca. 1914), 'The Waste Land,' and 'The Hollow-Men.'"

"There are several ways to escape from this world of profit and loss and materialism and hate, I suppose. Certain types of men have been doing it for years. I sometimes think the high point of my life, each year, is a week or so in retreat in a monastery. There I can read, I work in the small fields or in the kitchen, etc. But more important we begin and end the day—and break the work day 4 times—to go to the chapel to pray. There and there only is some kind of hope. In the field of art, poetry, the most recent expression of this is T. S. Eliot's "Four Quarters," published in 1943 in the midst of the War, when he was serving as an air raid guard in London.

"For some vague, possibly God-given, reason, we desire to live and desire peace in the midst of hate and war."

In replying to Mr. Lawrence, I said:

"I can appreciate your love of art, music, and meditation—I love them myself—but I would call your attention to the rejoinder Dr. Herman Kahn has given to those young people who would like to see us return to a state of nature akin to that of the Indians who inhabited this continent at the time it was first settled by Europeans. Dr. Kahn points out that the area that constitutes the United States was at that time populated by about two million Indians; and he says the land was barely adequate to support even that number. Today we have over two hundred million people living here. It is all very well to talk of living like the carefree Indian, but what do we do with the excess population of one hundred and ninety-eight million? Is it not the willingness of most of our people to work hard for material incentives that makes it possible for those who enjoy art, music, and meditation to do so in comfort and in unprecedented numbers?"

Honorable Sir: August 19, 1969

Your reply to young Marc was as near perfect as it could possibly be. I sent a copy to my oldest granddaughter.

93

This girl is exceptionally bright. She graduated as vale-
dictorian from Modesto Junior College. Two years ago, she
entered University of California at Berkeley and graduated
with honors this year. She comes from a strong Republican
family and was brought up in a solid Presbyterian environment. She is no "hippy"—has never been in a demonstration—has worked every summer in places like Penneys.

Enclosed is the reply that I requested. By this you can
see that our young folks that are exposed to present day university atmosphere are influenced by modern ways of thinking.

If you could find time in your busy schedule to read my
granddaughter's reply, I would appreciate it. I would be most
grateful if you would care to give me a reply.

Yours sincerely,
J. E. Kirkman
Madera, California

His granddaughter's letter was as follows:

August 9, 1969

Dear Grandpa,

I find it very difficult to try to comment on the article
without talking to you about it so I would know how deeply
you would like me to respond; nevertheless, I am proud you
are interested in what I might feel.

Perhaps the first thing I'd better say is that Mr. Robertson's style makes me angry. I think his subtle use of Marxian
or Communist examples as illustrations of the boy's point of
view is a gross exaggeration of the boy's statements. Mr.
Robertson invariably chooses from a wide range of possible
interpretations of the statements that one most calculated to
frighten his reading audience. An example of this is his discussion of excerpt No. 8. First, he puts words in the boy's
mouth. He says, "What you are saying is . . . ," and so limits his attack to this narrow understanding equating the boy

94

with Lenin, the end of democratic processes, the end of civil rights and especially that of ownership of property." If you will look at the boy's article, the next to the last paragraph, you will find he is not advocating totalitarianism, but the restoration in full of rights basic to men (or that seem to me to be), rights declared in the Constitution or by Congress.

Having thought about the article for about a week now, I no longer feel it is important for me to answer specifically the points I believe are false in Mr. R's article. In fact I often agree with what he is saying. I believe for instance that each man to a point has a right to every cent he earns, an inalienable right—which is one of the central points of Mr. R's article. I also firmly agree with him that the U.S. is a comparatively democratic and idealistic country which is comparatively good to its allies. Finally, I couldn't be more sure that material well-being is a blessing, not a curse. I am bothered, however, by the conclusions to which he takes these good beginnings. He seems to carry these facts to the conclusion that since material well being is a blessing, we should consider ourselves blessed and ignore the problems that it brings, ignore or deny them instead of working with them to make conditions in the U.S. even better. He seems to be saying that because we are a comparatively benevolent nation we should be happy and satisfied instead of facing and searching for remedies for the ills with which we are still plagued. I resent and am deeply hurt by his attitude of "America: Love it or Leave it," which seems to me to imply either accept it the way it is or get out. It seems to me that I love my country very much and the highest way I have of showing this is by desiring to make it even better, even more in line with its ideals. Our nation's freedom, equality, and personal rights require constant vigilance if they are to be kept intact. If I feel that one of these is being threatened for any American I will fight for it because I love my country, not because I want to destroy it!

Earlier I said it seemed to me that a man had an inalienable right to all his property to a point. I can think of two times when his right to sole control over his property might be modified. One of these would be that if he uses services or equipment provided, he should pay for that privilege. This means to me that men should contribute to the government which protects them, provides them with a postal system, highways, national parks, etc. I think this is obvious. The second exception is harder to explain. In the U.S., and I preface my explanation with that because it seems irrelevant to me what happens anywhere else in the world because nowhere else makes the claim of equality we do and nowhere else do I love or care about so. Anyway, in the U.S. I think there is a basic right, a right that all the others depend on and without which they won't work; this seems to me to be a right of impartiality. I believe this is a right which doesn't exist in many other countries, has been an unattained ideal throughout the history of this country, an ideal toward which we have been slowly moving and the one which now needs the people of America's most concentrated attention, one which must be made in actuality to be what our words as Americans have boasted that it is.

It is the right of every man to be judged the equal of every other until he proves himself to be more or less capable, intelligent, polite, kind or whatever. In our society **now** with the attitudes toward underprivileged people, whether "okies" or blacks or whoever, it has had, and I mean attitudes other than this one of impartiality, damage has been done. Young people my age have been treated partially; been told in high school they were fit only for trades, been allowed after high school janitorial jobs because, ". . . that was all they were fit for." People younger than I, say more Jamie's, William's, Johanna's age go to schools staffed with the new teachers in the district, inexperienced teachers because that is city policy, go to crowded schools because the city established districts in order to keep them isolated, are hated by their teachers because they can be monsters and the teachers have no understanding because no education in the conditions of these kids' lives.

This is not impartial education, or life in an impartial society and these kids are unable, are prevented from being judged impartially as adults by the too partial horror of their childhoods; adults are not treated impartially, on merit, but have their lives predestined by our society to want, to bitterness, to ignorance.

So this is my other exception to rights of property as absolute. The right of anyone to be born into a neutral—not actively menacing nor favorable world seems to me to be one that Americans have guaranteed **in words** to their children and must see becomes real. To me this means Head Start Programs supported in part by me; it means extra education and pay for ghetto teachers, it means black studies departments at Berkeley—to say in symbol to a black, "Yes, you too exist in the U.S." It means special concern with getting black adults jobs and seeing that they or **any** minority group has a representative voice in the governmental and economic shaping of their lives. Most of all I think it means less fear and distrust on our parts, on Mr. R's part.

When our fear of change makes us equate, as Mr. R. does, all change with Communism, when it makes us for instance take the words of the farthest leftists in the People's Park support group as indicating the feelings and beliefs of the entire group, and what is more, take these peoples able in their obvious negativeness and unconstructiveness to persuade and dupe such a large group of extremely intelligent Americans, then the fear is no longer based in fact or common sense and one needs to look again at human nature, to remember that these people are PEOPLE unknown to one, and not dupes nor demons.

I am so glad you wanted to communicate with me on this and I'd sure like to know how you feel about what I've written. I think such talking is so necessary, so much better than Mr. R's subtle and fear-motivated hints that the boy is "like" if not is a Communist, is so much better than the young people who fear you of the older generation and so speak hate filled words about destroying the University.

There cannot be a racial or economic self perpetuating class system in America and have it still be the America I am proud of. I feel deeply that what must be done is for each of us inside himself to search and find out if he isn't perpetuating such a class system by his predestining opinions and attitudes. When you and I and every other citizen of the U.S. has examined himself in such a manner, performed such an "American" activity, then I think America will be closer to what she has aimed to be, that much more to be proud of.

As I said, I argued with myself quite a while before deciding to reply to you generally rather than sticking specifically to the text of the article. I kind of feel like I have answered the questions behind the article, that if I debated Mr. R's facts and assertions point by point I might be able to prove him wrong, but this would be silly because he could find other facts to prove himself right and I wouldn't be letting you know how I felt anyway. I hope this is the kind of response you were looking for; I'm so happy you consider my opinion worth questioning and that you are as concerned as I about these problems. Such exchange of ideas is great. Hope to see you soon.

Love,
Genevieve

August 25, 1969

Dear Mr. Kirkman:

I am grateful to you for your letter, and I was particularly interested in your granddaughter Genevieve's critique of my reply to Marc Machiz. It is important that we give our young people the advantage of our experience and thinking, but it is also important to listen to them and analyze what they are saying.

I was sorry that what I said to Marc made Genevieve angry. It would have been more satisfying to have convinced her. However, the fact that she took the time to read the material and write a long comment on it shows that the lines of communication between the generations are open, and that is good. What is more, Genevieve indicates that she does agree with much of what I said, which means that we are probably not terribly far apart in our thinking. Indeed, I think that her disagreement with me is based largely on misunderstanding of my own position.

I would like to clarify for her sake the fact that I did not write to Marc with the intention of having the letter published. It is incorrect to assume that I was trying to frighten anyone or place him in a bad light. She will be interested to know that I have since had some very pleasant correspondence with Marc, and I think he fully appreciates what I was trying to do.

In restating Marc's sentence, "Human rights must be placed above both property and majority rights," I was merely pointing out what can logically be inferred from a high-sounding rhetorical statement. I am quite certain that many of our young people are captured by the seeming beauty of such phrases without fully appreciating what they really mean. I wanted Marc to look beyond the rhetoric and try to see the probable consequences of a program based on a deceptive slogan. Our schools should be teaching youngsters to analyze propaganda in this way.

I assume that Genevieve did not read my Omaha speech. Had she done so, she could hardly have concluded that my attitude was "America: love it or leave it." I think that she would also have understood that I am not one who thinks that our society is perfect and that criticism and dissent should be forcibly suppressed. I emphasized that we should not discourage the dreams of the idealists and the aspirations of youth. I pointed out that these are an important source of change and orderly progress. I also noted that our young people necessarily play an important role in transmitting our civilized values to future generations and that we cannot afford to write off a whole generation. I would certainly not want to see them fleeing from the United States. On the contrary, I want them to stay here and work to make this an even better country. But I also want to help them understand the ideas and values that have made this country as wonderful as it is. They will not build well if they destroy the foundation that has been laboriously constructed by their forebears at great cost. Nor will they build well if they lack both plans and understanding of the principles that must be followed to design workable plans for a sound social order.

It seems to me that Genevieve, like so many of our young people, assumes that the evils in the world are mainly traceable to the bad motives of other people, such as me, rather than to difficulties inherent in the problems to be solved. She assumes, incorrectly, that I am not interested in solutions to the problems of racial injustice and poverty. She implies that our "racial or self-perpetuating class system" can be overcome if each individual will only undertake to examine and reform his own attitude.

Of course, if all men were angels we would have heaven on earth. But all men are not angels and no mortal man has yet discovered a way of making them so. Some have thought that this could be done by killing enough of the bad ones that those who were left would be terrorized into behaving just as the rulers wanted. Eric Hoffer has referred to these as "soul engineers who want to operate on mankind with an ax." So far, the results of this approach have never been very agreeable.

The problems associated with differences in income and different racial and cultural backgrounds are complex and terribly difficult. Changing attitudes can ameliorate them. Anyone who has lived in Washington for the past 40 years, as I have, must be impressed by the degree to which attitudes on race have changed. However, in spite of the great progress that has been made in eliminating discriminatory practices, we must recognize that in recent years we have experienced an increase in racial tension and conflict. Genevieve is too young to remember, but almost no one believed a decade ago that the great strides that have been made in civil rights legislation in the last ten years would be accompanied by a deterioration in race relations and a growing movement for black separatism. Perhaps this can be explained logically, but the fact remains that it was not foreseen by very many people. I cite this only to make the point that the solution to the problem was not as simple as many people assumed ten years ago. It may not be as simple as Genevieve and many of her generation assume today.

In any case, I think we are entitled to ask these youngsters not to impugn our motives and not to blame the ills of the world on our bad character. No doubt many of our generation were guilty of doing this when we were very young. We have learned, as Genevieve will learn, that it is not quite that simple. And sometimes one can, in spite of good intentions, make things worse. That was what I was trying to tell Marc.

Sincerely,
J. L. Robertson

The following letter was forwarded to me by Mr. David Lawrence, Editor, *U.S. News and World Report*, at the request of Mr. Lowell Ponte:

Mr. David Lawrence:

The recent dialogue "One Generation Speaks to Another" in your July 7th issue presented two cogent view-
points. By printing both you have doubtless helped enlighten
many members of each of the generations spoken for. As a
graduate student and one of the earliest issue of the Postwar
Baby Boom, however, I found my perspective somehow akin
with, yet alien to, both views presented, and I contribute this
view from the gapping generation in the hope of adding some
ruts and crevices to the issues considered.

Marc Machiz, a New York high school student who
claims to hold "radical beliefs," points to a few social and political inequities in contemporary America and blames those
inequities on the "materialism" he sees at the root of traditional American values. James L. Robertson, Vice Chairman
of the Federal Reserve Board, answers Machiz's charges by
denying some, ignoring others, and by asserting that property rights, vital to human rights, should be preserved even
as property in America is more equitably distributed. Seen
thus, the dialogue appears confused because both sides are in
large part correct—not paradoxically, since Mr. Machiz,
lacking a precise plan for change, is not a radical, and Mr.
Robertson, choosing government power as an appropriate
means for the advancement of his vague humanism, is not a
capitalist. Both belong together on the delicate spectrum of
democratic fascism that has become the **sine qua non** of
modern American society.

By way of explanation, a few issues need to be clari-
fied:

1. **Fascism:** The term is mine, and I introduce it in the
recognition that it carries ugly and distorting connotations. I
use the term, however, to emphasize its economic rather
than political aspects. To simplify, fascism is a social system

in which the government leaves the means of production in the hands of private owners—thus encouraging individual incentives for gain—but in which the government retains strong controls over how individuals may use their property. No businessman in America will deny that today the government has a staggering range of controls. Businesses are subject to various levels of licensing, taxation, inspection, compulsory bargaining, worker compensation regulations, price restraints, and other controls. Most of this government activity is conducted through bureaucratic agencies, the employees of which are civil servants insulated from the pressures of electoral politics. Even the least of these agencies can cause an individual company acute difficulties; most could, with little effort on their part, harass most companies out of business. It is interesting to recall that prominent among Thomas Jefferson's charges against King George III in the Declaration of Independence was that the mad monarch had sent hordes of bureaucrats and tax collectors among the people.

Just as a fascist government can destroy its foes, so it can reward its friends. Thus sectors of the American economy which in another time would have decried government excesses are today bought off with lucrative government grants and contracts. When government defense spending alone accounts for 10 per cent of GNP—as it does in the U.S. today—one can only gasp at the government's manipulative potential. With each new reward goes a new thread in the tangled web of governmental restriction, and the resulting shroud is really neither democratic nor capitalist.

2. **Materialism:** Mr. Machiz asserts that "The idea that everyone is entitled to what is his and a chance to obtain more is the underlying principle behind American democracy." Mr. Robertson answers rightly that this has not necessarily led to a preoccupation with material wealth for

its own sake; he notes, moreover, that society has always assumed the right to tax individuals, and that "the personal right to property can be legitimately curtailed to the extent necessary to provide support to those who are unable to support themselves." More than one out of seven Americans today is a government employee, the salaries and operating costs for which come out of taxes; would these employees, one wonders, be otherwise unable to support themselves? Because of a proliferation of government regulation and taxation, most individuals are increasingly dependent on their government; will the day come, one wonders, when the government will tax all people into poverty or regulate them into helplessness so that it may legitimately declare how incapable they are of caring for themselves?

The value of American "materialism," subtly misunderstood by both Machiz and Robertson, is that material gain or regulative distance provided for individuals the obverse of threat; to be secure financially, or to be distant from government regulation, was traditionally to be secure politically—to be relatively independent of political influence or, at least, to be able to fight back with political influence of one's own. With emphasis placed thus, Robertson's assertion of the centralness of property rights to human rights takes on a vivid correctness. With emphasis placed thus, Machiz's objections to America's material and social inequities take on a new importance—for in today's America the growing cooperation between business and government has tended towards a fascist synthesis which can easily afford to buy off or bypass the will of the people and thus stifle democracy. As Hans Morgenthau recently observed, power in the United States is flowing at an alarming rate away from the people and into the hands of governmental bureaucracy—a complex nowadays almost unamenable to democratic influence. Mr. Robertson, fond of quoting Yugoslav Milovan Djilas, would do well to read his "The New Class," a consideration of how such bureaucratic systems undermine all idealistic societies, communist and capitalist alike.

3. **Progress and Freedom:** Our present government seeks to move Americans into certain narrow channels of thought. One such channel is the "problem-solution" orientation, which makes one say: "Unless you have a **practical** solution to a problem, assume that 'WE' are working on one and shut up! Don't cry out in pain and cause needless tensions!" The second channel is that of consensus—the determination which, among other things, is the criterion for what is "practical"—the nature of which is suggested by Mr. Robertson's objection to those who "exaggerate and distort the facts in order to prove a point," his reason being that their vocalization "creates conflict and tension because people who have a different understanding of the facts will probably reach very different conclusions and will advocate different policies." And so we see that a goal of Mr. Robertson's America is homogeneity of opinion, a comfortable agreement as to what "facts" mean. Very nice—for "1984." But it was in this spirit in 1962 that Deputy Secretary of Defense Arthur Sylvester bragged openly of news management and distortion, calling it a permanent and active part of U.S. government policy. In such a society, "democracy" is itself a tool of consensus used by the government, not a tool of government correction available to the people.

A third channel of thought derived from our fascist government is a derivative in turn of CATCH-22, the fact that "THEY" can do anything to you that you cannot keep them from doing. "You," as an individual, soon learn that "you" cannot do much and that to try to prevail against the system is to be crushed. Conversely, to cooperate with the system is to be upheld, to be led to success and social security.

An ugly symptom of this idea is the Selective Service

System. Mr. Robertson suggests that young men object to the draft because they consider America unworthy of defense. I know many draft resisters and am convinced that if America were attacked and if Congress issued a declaration of war that almost all young men would eagerly join in her defense. Perhaps Mr. Robertson fought for his country when its aims were made clear by such a Congressional declaration, when wartime objectives were defined and unequivocal, when Americans died but did so indubitably in defense of **vital** American interests. In those days the draft was not a "peace-time" thing and was not used as a device of coercion to—in the word of the present Director of the Selective Service System—"rechannel" young men's lives into jobs and activities deemed useful and acceptable to the government. Such manipulation of young lives may be pragmatically justifiable in terms of future material output to the nation, but it represents an end of the freedoms that this country's Founding Fathers fought and died for.

Is it time for another revolution? Yes—at least in the attitudes of individuals towards themselves and their government. People need to alter drastically their way of thinking, such that the government is compelled to restore a respect for individual dignity. As Eric Hoffer suggested, speaking recently of university administrators, people must again be animated by a dymanic recognition of their rights, both to their property and to their persons. They must, as Hoffer said, be willing to die if need be in the defense of those rights—whether the threat to them comes from vocal mobs or from government itself.

Mr. Machiz called for rapid change, and my recommendation above is suggested . . . a change of minds. Mr. Robertson, in his June 9th editorial in "U.S. News" told a story of a truck driver's retaliation against a maurauding gang of motorcycle-riding thugs; I suggest that he re-read it, recognizing that contemporary government must be seen as the thugs, the thieves of private property rights, the perpetrators of terror. It is high time the American people reacted accordingly.

A closing note on "1984," an analogy used by Mr. Robertson. Both generations bordering on "the gap" should realize that the world of Big Brother's totalitarianism came about, in Orwell's depiction, not by a revolution but by a mobilization of the forces of "law and order" in the name of "the people's own good." Its mobilization was maintained by directing public energies into foreign wars and by compelling military service—this in the name of patriotism. Its watchword was consensus, and its method was news management. I leave it up to the reader to draw those parallels which seem appropriate.

Lowell Ponte
Redlands, California

July 18, 1969

Dear Mr. Ponte:

I have read your paper written in response to the exchange of correspondence between Marc Machiz and myself.

I wish that it were possible to reply to all of the letters that I have received that raise substantial issues in detail. Time does not permit this, and I will have to confine myself to a few remarks on your interesting paper.

I am sorry that you did not ponder a little more carefully the passage in my letter in which I criticized those who exaggerate and distort the facts in order to prove a point. You appear to have interpreted this to mean that I was advocating a homogeneity of opinion enforced by totalitarian methods.

You are the only person of the scores who have written to me who has suggested that there is something wrong in recommending that we all strive to avoid adding to the supply of lies, distortions and exaggerations that exist in the world. There are plenty of areas in which hard factual information is lacking and there is ample room for value judgments even when the facts are known without confusing matters even more by deliberately ignoring facts and falsifying information.

One way of distorting and exaggerating is by the semantic method. Confucius was once asked what he would do if he were made governor of a certain province. He said that the first thing he would do would be to make sure that everything was called by its right name, otherwise there would be endless confusion. When one calls our form of political and economic organization "fascist" one applies a name that is normally used to describe a system that is very different from the one we have. You may recall that Abraham Lincoln once asked his son how many legs a dog would have if you called a tail a leg. The boy replied, "Five." "No," said Lincoln, "just calling a tail a leg doesn't make it a leg."

Calling our system "fascist" doesn't make it fascist; it just confuses. This confusion seems evident in your own paper. Having applied a term that suggests the existence of a totalitarian form of government, you proceed to attribute to our government far greater domination over the affairs of the residents of this country than actually exists. I am amazed at the tendency to attribute omnipotence to the "establishment" and the "military-industrial complex" at the very moment when a major decision made by the President and favored by the military and the industries supplying the military is in serious danger of being rejected in a Senate vote.[1] I cannot quite picture that happening in Hitler's

---

[1] A reference to the Safeguard anti-ballistic missile authorization which was approved by the Senate by a very narrow margin.

Germany, Mussolini's Italy, or any other totalitarian or authoritarian state.

Arthur Koestler signalled his defection from the Communist Party by including in a speech to a party meeting this statement: '"A harmful truth is better than a useful lie."

If you want to avoid totalitarianism, as your paper suggests, I would think you would want to adopt that as a slogan, for totalitarianism cannot succeed without deception. But you cannot very well insist that others adhere rigorously to the truth and at the same time maintain that you yourself have no obligation to do so.

Sincerely,

J. L.   Robertson

July 23, 1969

Dear Mr. Robertson:

Thank you for your comments concerning my response to the dialogue between Mr. Machiz and yourself.

I write to you again to clarify some of the confusions apparently caused you. First, concerning fascism: I defined the term with a specific economic emphasis, the use of which differentiating it from—

(a) capitalism, in which individuals and corporations own private property and can use both that property and the profit made by its use as they see fit; and

(b) socialism, in which the means of production are owned outright by the government.

Fascism, I specified, existed when private property existed, but did so only when the property owners adhered to a vast range of government control.

Of the three systems above mentioned, all three can be "democratic," can hold elections and be responsive to the "will of the people." None is **a priori** totalitarian. Moreover, the three styles can mix, as in modern America; in the United States the government owns an enormous amount of property and production facilities, yet it permits individuals many areas of freedom in their personal lives. It is only when individuals try to use their freedom through property that the potential and actual mechanisms of government control become painfully apparent to them—as you and I both know very well. I use the term fascist in reference to this extensive control both because it is accurate in a strict semantic sense (in keeping with your policy of using a right word for everything) and because it suggests the capability for social control held by government.

One such power I suggested—looking back to a statement by Deputy Defense Secretary Sylvester made in 1962—was that of news management.

As you must realize, Mr. Robertson, **facts** are not handed down like divine Platonic essences. **Facts** are those things on which a majority of people agree exist, presumably in the empirical world. Since my concern in the first place was with the political world, a world already built on emotion and illusion, discussions of the empirical world are peripheral to the issue. Even so, I suggest that you re-read "1984" or "Brave New World" to see some of the more blatant devices of making public perceptions uniform. A state does not have to have absolute agreement on issues among its people so long as it can manipulate their perceptions, make their recognition of the "facts" similar. When you say that people lie about or distort the "facts," what you mean is that for some reason their perception seems to differ from yours; perhaps this apparent difference stems from evil in their hearts, but perhaps too it derives from preconceptions in your head.

The most sophisticated types of government control are those which present the illusion of freedom, and in a democratic society this illusion is accompanied often by a degree of real freedom. People can be free to speak their minds so long as their perceptions are dominated by their government; dissent can be tolerated so long as it doesn't threaten the basic precepts of the system, "break the laws," or translate itself into action. If carefully used, in fact, dissent can be pointed to by government as a proof of freedom in the society, as indeed it is. For you to point to the ABM debate as a symbol of freedom, however, is most strange; it is an intergovernmental dispute, the outcome of which will be little affected by the will of the people. I can agree wholeheartedly with your precept that the truth would be a good thing for all of us. How would you, in a few words, define America's present economic system? Capitalist?

Sincerely yours,
Lowell Ponte
Redlands, California

July 30, 1969

Dear Mr. Ponte:

Thank you for your letter of July 23rd. It is my impression that you attribute to the government practices and goals which are more characteristic of the world of advertising than government.

There are exceptions to every generalization, but from my long experience in government I can honestly say that agencies of the United States Government do conscientiously endeavor to see that the factual information that they publish is accurate and complete. The stastistical information published by the Federal Reserve, for example, is not compiled with the objective of convincing anyone of anything. It may be used by Federal Reserve officials to demonstrate that our policies have been wise, or it may be used by our critics to demonstrate that they have been unwise. The members of the Board would be the first to criticize the staff if the data that were published were inaccurate or misleading.

While there are many items of information about whose accuracy honest men may differ, there are many things that we can ascertain beyond reasonable doubt. For example, the Federal Reserve discount rate is a perfectly knowable fact at any given time. But it is also possible for people to be mistaken about the rate and to draw false conclusions based on their misinformation. What I have tried to emphasize is that we can reduce tension if we will all make a sincere effort to check our facts before jumping to conclusions.

Government by definition means restriction of absolute freedom. Its absence would be anarchy. That has never been found a very agreeable arrangement for long. I would describe our present economic system as a liberal free market economy subject to a moderate degree of governmental regulation.

Sincerely   yours,

J.   L.   Robertson

June 30, 1969

Dear Mr. Robertson:

After reading the letter written to you by Marc Machiz, I decided to answer some of the dangerous contradictions in his letter myself. However, before doing so I read your reply which compelled me to write to you instead.

The substance of my letter to Marc was to be that it is inconsistent and contradictory to support "the right to freedom from invasion of privacy by our governmental institutions" and, at the same time, to support the right of the government to distribute property (money) by whatever means it chooses.

I did not write that letter because I feel that you have weakened the free enterprise system (capitalism) more than Marc could in his adamant opposition to it; in your "defense" of capitalism you have neglected those things which make it the only system which supports the rights of the individual and have instead supported some of the characteristics of our economy (which is not pure capitalism) which are causing problems throughout our system. I do not have sufficient ability to clarify the issue to the extent which I would wish, but I will attempt to point out a few of the inconsistencies.

America's spiritual development is, in large measure, dependent upon economic freedom. Such freedom stimulates the competition of ideas and of art and guarantees the originator credit for his discovery. It encourages what is best and noblest, in the true sense of the word, through the same competition. Historically economic rights have stood with freedom of speech in importance; one of the chief grievances leading to the Revolutionary War was the interference of Great Britain in the American economy by means of the various Navigation Acts. Also, economic rights (property rights) were at least as important as those spiritual in the settling of America; the issue was also tax support of the Church of England.

You were correct in your second comment to Marc if you meant that freedom was not the result of capitalism (democracy can be a tyranny); capitalism only exists in free societies. Therefore, it could not change another society to one of freedom because it could not exist in the one which was not free. It is interesting to note, however, that Marc linked the two. I wonder, though, that he does not seem to realize that if one controls capitalism one also must, as a matter of cause and effect, control freedom. Obviously, freedom cannot be controlled without destroying it. The consequence of economic control seems evident.

I propose to consider next Marc's statement "Our institutions don't have the capability to adjust." You seem confident that they can; I must disagree. Our institutions (in their present state) do seem to be in difficulty. There is a widespread denial of any authority, an increasing acceptance of violence as a tool for change, and an increasing, and disturbing, lack of genuine competence on all levels of society. However, the causes of these problems do not lie in economic

113

freedom, but in economic controls. The attempt to "tinker" with the economy (and I am not speaking merely of the last few months) restricts the business community from pursuing its interests, which are also those of all free men. Controls make unprofitable businesses profitable and handicap those which make profits because of ability, competence.

My final comment will be exceedingly brief: Human rights cannot be placed above property rights because the right to the disposal of the fruits of one's efforts (property) is one of the most fundamental of individual rights. We cannot destroy one individual right without gravely endangering all of them; we cannot control freedom without destroying it.

I, too, am a radical student, though not in the same way as many today. I believe strongly in individual rights; I also will protect them, all of them, to the best of my ability. (If you are interested I will be a freshman at Yale University this fall.)

Sincerely,
Anne E. Chafer
Oklahoma City, Oklahoma

July 17, 1969

Dear Miss Chafer:

One of the nice results of the publication of my correspondence with Marc Machiz is that it has brought to my attention the fact that we have a lot of young people in this country who are articulate and intelligent. I appreciate your taking the time and trouble to write your critique of my letter. I hope you will write to Marc as well.

I cannot see that your views and mine are very far apart. As I explained in my letter to Marc, I regard the right to own private property as a fundamental human right. You make a valid point in showing that there is a link between economic freedom and other freedoms, but I think you overstate the degree to which modifications of economic freedom impinge upon both the functioning of the economic machine and the enjoyment of human rights. I have had considerable experience with various types of governmental controls over the economy, and I would agree that many times they do more harm than good. However, the economic machinery is pretty resilient and it has been demonstrated that it will take more abuse than the purists generally realize. The pressure to have the government intervene to solve this or that defect is often irresistible. It is not necessary to lose all hope because such controls are adopted. The problem in a democratic society such as ours frequently becomes one of trying to persuade a majority of the people that you have reason on your side. As a practical matter, this cannot be done by a blanket condemnation of all government intervention in the economy. Sometimes it is pretty hard to do even when it can be demonstrated that the intervention is having a specific harmful effect that outweighs its advantages.

It is too much to expect perfection in our society, because we are committed to a system based on compromise. All of us will have to put up with some things we do not like. That is the price we pay to avoid being subject to dictatorship.

Sincerely,

J. L.   Robertson

July 3, 1969

Dear Mr. Robertson:

It was with great interest that I read the exchange of letters between Marc Machiz and yourself, which letters the "U.S. News and World Report" interpret as covering the question "should the American system be torn down for one that would put human rights above property rights?"

It seems to me that the question as posed does not call for the real answers to the generation gap. In my opinion the real generation gap is a feeling of mistrust and lack of confidence in the establishment.

I believe that many of our young people have a subconscious feeling that we in America are approaching a crisis of great economic, spiritual and moral consequences, and the establishment will not, with its attitude and fixations, be able to satisfactorily handle the crisis without great waste of human and natural resources.

I believe you are inclined to give the materialistic element of our people credit for the survival of our democratic form of government, where, in fact, the credit should be given to its founders, who, under great stress, were so inspired that they devised a system that has prevailed in spite of the materialists.

There is no question in my mind that the great natural and human resources of this country have sustained us to this point in time, in spite of the great waste and destruction of same in the quest for material wealth.

Following are a few of the many conditions that I believe create this feeling of mistrust:

How can you reconcile in a young man's mind, and many older heads I might add, the spectacle of our leaders (Congressmen, Senators, Industrialists, Union Leaders, etc.) fattening their pocketbooks indiscriminately and at the same time sending young people to war in a foreign country to sacrifice the most precious thing that any of us have—"life."

Thousands of our citizens in all walks of life, but predominantly of the older generations, systematically swindling our government.

Inequitable tax systems.

Inefficient transportation systems.

Deliberate fouling of our environment in the cause of profit.

Waste of natural resources in the name of profit.

Inefficient and immoral system of justice.

There seems to be no end to the items that could be added to this list, and the terrible realization of it all is that the guilty people are generally ones that have been well educated, are members in high standing in the various religious and business establishments, and enjoy the honors and privileges of high public office.

What a mess of hypocrisy! What bad examples are being set!

It may be that some day future generations will realize that our present day dissenters, violent and non-violent, will have saved our democratic form of government.

It is my feeling that many of our people in high places economically, spiritually, and politically will conclude, if they take time to really examine their past performances, that they have been very unpatriotic and disloyal to our form of government—that is if they really care.

Of course, much of what I say here is based on conclusions reached by perusing our various forms of public press and communication; but then, these sources of information may also be inaccurate, inefficient or untrue and I am, therefore, the victim of circumstances and what might be called misguided.

Sincerely,

L. W. Lepping
Philadelphia, Pennsylvania

July 17, 1969

Dear Mr. Lepping:

It was good of you to take the time and trouble to comment on my letter to Marc Machiz.

You state that I give the materialistic element of our people credit for the survival of our democratic form of government. If you will look at the paragraphs under No.2 in my letter to Marc Machi, YOU WILL SEE THAT I said exactly the opposite.

I cannot disagree with what you say about many of the obvious flaws in our social and political system creating tension and distrust. But I think we should remember what Winston Churchill said about democracy—that it is the worst form of government in the world, except for all others.

I referred in my letter to March Machiz to Milovan Djilas' book, "The Unperfect Society." Djilas explained that he used the word "unperfect" deliberately because he wanted to convey the idea that perfection was not really possible.

Where I differ from some of our young people is that I believe in trying to improve on what we have rather than destroying it and starting all over again. If we have inequitable tax systems, let us work to make them more equitable, but we may have to recognize that what you regard as equitable will be considered grossly inequitable by others. If our transport systems are inefficient, let us try to make them more efficient, not blow them up.

I join with you in hoping that our younger generation will save our democratic form of government, even though it be less than perfect. This is what I have urged them to do. The ones I worry about are those who proclaim their intention to destroy democracy and civil liberties and set up a dictatorial regime that will usher in a new era of righteousness. The world has had its fill of righteous tyrants intent on creating Utopias.

Sincerely,
J. L. Robertson

part **6**

more critics: economics, politics, race, and the role of ideas

A number of the letters that I received were from people whose comments were focused on specific issues such as poverty, race, foreign investment, and the policy of the United States toward dictatorships abroad. These were from individuals who did not question our fundamental values but who were perplexed by some seeming inconsistencies between the values we profess and our actions.

I have endeavored in my replies to explain something about the achievements that we have to our credit, while recognizing that we frequently fall far short of perfection. I confess that I have some difficulty understanding why the treatment of the American Indians from the 17th through the 19th centuries has become such a burning issue with some of our young people. It appears that the children *wish* to suffer for the alleged sins of their great-grandparents, but they do not wish to take the trouble to place themselves in the position of the pioneers who opened up a wild continent to civilization. One can admire the humanitarian sentiments that are reflected in the mourning for the mistreatment of human beings by other human beings in the past; but, to quote Shakespeare, "What is gone is past help and should be past grief." We cannot right all the wrongs of past centuries. We should concentrate on righting those of our own time. I am not at all impressed by the humanitarianism of those who can work up no indignation about the denial of freedom and human dignity to millions in Eastern Europe, Communist China and Cuba, but who lacerate their consciences over the sins of their ancestors.

One letter that I wish I had answered at greater length was the one from Mr. R. V. Brandborg of Little Falls, Minnesota. I responded very briefly to his lengthy exposition of the Marxian materialistic interpretation of history. This was mainly because I had no expectation that anything that I might say would shake this mature individual's acceptance of this way of looking at the world. Had I thought that my response would reach a wider audience, I would have dealt with the issue differently.

The doctrine that Mr. Brandborg expounds has had a tremendous influence on the thinking of many Americans who would stoutly deny any affinity for the ideas of Karl Marx. I alluded to this in my comment to Marc Machiz about the influence of historian Charles A. Beard and his theory of the economic interpretation of the Constitution of the United States. The Marxian notion is that the key to all historical development is to be found in economic relationships. If you give a young student who knows almost nothing about economics or history this simple key, there is a danger that he will immediately think that he has a better grasp of history, past, present, and future, than any scholar who is not in on the secret.

There are many ways to demonstrate that the "key" is not the valuable instrument that those who use it pretend. The simplest is to challenge its use as a predictive device, which is what I did in my letter to Mr. Brandborg. Marx and Engels, the discoverer of this supposed great key to the understanding of the historical process, were surely among the worst prophets the world has ever seen. They were certain that the evolution of capitalism would result in ever increasing misery for the workers and that this would explode into a revolution that would make 1793 look like child's play. At one point Engels said this could be foretold for England with almost mathematical certainty. We know, of course, that things did not work out as these prophets foretold. Normally, when a scientific hypothesis does not work as a predictive tool, it is discarded. In this case, however, it was clung to with ferocious determination.

Strangely enough, it was discarded by the leaders of the Marxist-Leninist movement in the world, but it has continued to influence the thinking of the non-Marxists. The Marxist-Leninists have long recognized that the world is moved by ideas. This is why they devote so much of their energy to propaganda work—the dissemination of ideas. They realize perfectly well that if they sat by and waited for the supposedly inevitable collapse of capitalism and the dawn of the Marxist-Leninist revolution that Marx predicted, they would wait forever. They know that it is by indoctrination and agitation, and in some cases aggressive wars and terrorism, that their kind of revolution is made. This is why they devote so much effort expanding their influence in institutions that can help disseminate ideas in areas where they are not in power.

Paradoxically, one of the ideas they assiduously spread is that ideas do not matter—that only economic relationships, environmental conditions influence human behavior. This is as if one contestant in the Indianapolis 500 tried to convince all his competitors that their racing cars would function better on prune juice than on high test gasoline, while putting only high test in his own tank. The analogy sounds absurd, but it is no more absurd than the reality of what has happened to our thinking about the relative importance of ideas and environment in determining how human beings behave. We have reached the stage where a very large segment of our brightest people accept the idea that ideas do not matter. They believe that crime is caused mainly by poverty, all wars by greed, racial discrimination by economic motives, etc. Hence, we have banked heavily upon what might be called the environmental solution to our social problems and we have seen those problems grow worse in many cases. We have neglected the role of

121

thinking, the role of ideas, apparently forgetting that it is precisely this that distinguishes man from the dumb animals.

Here are the letters:

September 4, 1969

Dear Mr. Robertson:

Your letter to Marc Machiz evaded a couple of his important points.

Marc made a mistake in saying that millions starve in this country, but what he probably meant was that millions live in poverty. You attacked his statement about starvation, but you did not tackle the underlying question of poverty. If our economic system is so wonderful, why do we have so much poverty in the midst of plenty?

Marc also made a reference to discrimination against the Negroes. He did not make a big point of this, but I don't think you can really communicate with **my** generation unless you can explain why your generation has so long tolerated the twin evils of poverty and racism.

> Sincerely yours,
> Beryl Andrus
> Bell, California

October 29, 1969

Dear Miss Andrus:

You are correct in noting that in my letter to Marc Machiz I focused more on the question of starvation than on the general question of poverty in America.

America is accused of tolerating massive poverty in the midst of plenty. This is a very old charge. Even before I was born, an American named Henry George wrote a book entitled "Progress and Poverty," which made him famous. It was his contention that poverty was actually increasing as we made economic progress. Looking back now, we can see that since his day we have made tremendous economic prog-

ress. **In terms of the standards that prevailed at the beginning of this century,** I think we might fairly say that we have
virtually eliminated poverty. Families who are classed as
poor today are able to enjoy many material goods that were
not even available to the rich seventy years ago. Things like
radio and television simply did not exist. There were no electric refrigerators, and there were precious few automobiles
and telephones, to name but a few of the comforts of life that
are widely enjoyed these days, even by families wholly dependent upon public welfare for their maintenance.

This points up the fact that one of the difficulties we face
in trying to eliminate poverty completely is that we keep
raising our standards. Poverty is a relative concept. It is also
in part a mental attitude. Shakespeare wrote, " 'Tis the mind
that makes the body rich." I have known many people with
low incomes who would have deeply resented being told they
were living in poverty. They were too proud to be poor. They
may have been down, but they were not out. But there are
those who are more easily overwhelmed by adversity. Their
circumstances may be aggravated by their tendency to give
up the struggle, perhaps to resign themselves to a life lacking
in dignity, perhaps taking refuge in alcohol or some other
means of escape from reality.

This is an important reason why poverty persists in our
affluent country. It is not that we tolerate it, any more than
we tolerate cancer or heart disease. We simply have not yet
been able to overcome the root causes. As is true with cancer,
we do not really understand the causes.

Of course, to the extent that poverty is merely the word
we apply to describe the condition of those at the bottom of
the economic ladder, we can eliminate it only by providing
everyone with virtual equality of income. We can make the
lowest income groups absolutely better off, but they will still
be low income groups as long as anyone earns more than they
do.

In recent years we have seen the launching of a war on poverty by the government. The objective was to eliminate poverty, but as we look back after the expenditure of several billion dollars, we have to admit that the degree of success has not been overwhelming. While it has been said that the cure for poverty is money, that is not literally true. We have discovered that the expenditure of large sums of money can be like aspirin: it can suppress the pain without curing the disease.

I have no doubt that we will continue to spend large sums of money both to alleviate want and to try to find ways of getting at the root causes of poverty. But I would also like to suggest that our economic system, based on free enterprise, has been our best anti-poverty program. It has produced a degree of affluence in our society that is unprecedented in history and unmatched in the world. Indeed, there are some who think that the problems created by our affluence are as serious as the problems created by our residue of poverty.

It would be folly to attack this system that has worked so well simply because it has not ushered in a Utopia. Take a careful look at the alternative systems that are sometimes cited as models that we might emulate by those who advocate revolutionary change. Not only are they far inferior to the United States in economic performance and the equitable distribution of material goods, but what is worse, they deny man his freedom and dignity. The virtue of the American system is that it is predicated upon the idea that human freedom is conducive to material progress, not a barrier to it. Our success demonstrates that this idea is fundamentally sound. Those who have promised to bury us by regimenting their people and denying them the opportunity and incentive to exercise their talents as free men have stumbled badly.

I hope that your generation will build a country that will raise our material standards even higher, but I hope that in doing so you will not underestimate the value of your heritage of freedom.

Your second criticism of my generation is that we have tolerated racism. It is certainly true that we have long had racial discrimination in this country. It is no less true that we have been bending our energies toward its elimination. I find it strange that precisely at the time when we are making significant progress in this direction we find ourselves beset with unprecedented feelings of guilt. There was a time when Americans took great pride in the fact that we had accomplished the impossible in molding into a great nation a most diverse collection of men and women with widely varying ethnic, linguistic, cultural, and economic backgrounds. This is a feat of considerable importance. Granting that we have not done a perfect job as yet, few, if any, countries have done it better.

We can surely take pride in the fact that it is not our official policy to condone or encourage discrimination against any of the diverse ethnic or religious groups that make up our nation. Indeed, we have expanded the scope of our government's powers to actively combat such discrimination.

Contrast this with the situation that prevails in many other countries which are made up of diverse ethnic groups. You are familiar, I am sure, with the severe official policy of racial separation practiced in South Africa. You may recall the bitter war that broke out between the Greeks and Turks who inhabit Cyprus. For several years there has been a cruel repression of the Negro inhabitants of southern Sudan by the dominant Arabs in the north. In Zanzibar the reverse happened, with the Negroes killing and imprisoning the Arabs. In Nigeria, we find another bitter clash between people of the same race but representing different tribes and cultures.

In many countries in Asia the Chinese are a substantial minority, and they are frequently discriminated against and

125

Robertson: *"We can take pride in the fact that it is not our official policy to condone or encourage discrimination against any of the diverse ethnic or religious groups that make up our nation. . . . Contrast this with the situation that prevails in many other countries. . . ."*

Soviet Major General Piotr Grigorenko was arrested in 1969 for publicly protesting the official persecution of a minority racial group, the Tatars, in the USSR. General Grigorenko is shown here talking to newsmen about the trial of five Russians arrested for demonstrating against the Soviet invasion of Czechoslovakia.

—UPI PHOTO

sometimes violently persecuted. There was a tremendous bloodletting as a result of clashes between Moslems and Hindus at the time India and Pakistan received their independence from Britain, and the animosity between these two groups has resulted in more bloodshed in recent years. The Chinese communists have treated the Tibetans and other minority groups with great brutality and no regard for their religion and traditions.

The U.S.S.R. has boasted of its fair treatment of minority groups, but the boasts have been exposed as gross falsehoods in recent years. Anti-semitism has been shown to be officially encouraged in the Soviet Union. It has been made difficult for the Jews to perpetuate their religion and language. Victims of persecution and discrimination have ranged from members of the Ukrainian nation, one of the largest in the Soviet Union, to the Tatars, one of the smallest ethnic groups. The latter were torn from their homes in the Crimea during World War II, and to this day they have found it impossible to return and re-establish themselves. Those who have protested their condition have been arrested.

As one looks around the world, the realization grows that racial and national conflicts are extremely difficult problems with which to cope We, at least, are trying to iron out the problems, not aggravate them.

We cannot give you a perfect world, but in terms of the two criteria you cite, poverty and racism, my generation is certainly turning over to yours a better America than the one we inherited from our parents.

I hope that your generation will build on what has already been accomplished, not destroy the foundation because the edifice has not yet been completed to your satisfaction.

Sincerely,

J. L. Robertson

Dear Mr. Robertson:

Let me first express my approval of your concern in answering the letter from the young man from Great Neck who claimed that America's values were "worn out." I approve of your decision to answer him but I would be less than honest if I agreed with your answer.

Like you, I despise the brutality of the Soviet Regime. In citing the murder of the Kulaks, you are quite correct, and you also might have cited the virtual extermination of the Kalmuks, an Asiatic minority group which was wiped out almost completely after World War II because they allied themselves with the Axis against the Soviet Army. I note, however, that in deference to history, you might at least touch upon America's genocidal wars against the American Indian and our senseless and illegal incarceration of Japanese-Americans.

Of the former case, one can only conclude that it is the most shameful case study of brutality and greed ever recorded on the North American continent. The noble pilgrim fathers whose sacred memory we evoke every Thanksgiving once surrounded a village of sleeping Narrangansett Indians, set the village on fire and shot or spitted on pikes every Indian who attempted to escape.

"By the grace of God . . . " a pilgrim noted with Eichmannesque relish . . . "there were 200 more Indians biding ye night for a feast, so that we slew 500 of ye enemy at no great cost to ourselves." Over two hundred years later, in the Victorian era which agonized over the original Uncle Tom and sent missionaries to convert the yellow heathens of China and Japan, the Seventh U.S. cavalry slaughtered half of the last remaining band of Dakota Sioux Indians at Wounded Knee Creek. A doctor who arrived on the scene shortly after the glorious triumph pointed out that many of the women and girls of this band could still be seen exactly as they fell, with

Koester: *". . . you might at least touch upon America's genocidal wars against the American Indian. . . ."*

Robertson: *". . . the policies of the European settlers, harsh though they were in many cases . . . were far from genocidal."*

This painting by Charles Schreynagel depicts a cavalry attack on an Indian camp.

—COURTESY: LIBRARY OF CONGRESS

their shawls pulled over their faces so as not to see the soldiers who shot them in the backs of the head at point blank range. Thus, as General Sheridan put it, did our first Americans become "good" Indians.

Our incarceration of the Nisei, or Japanese Americans, is less gory but a great deal more stupid. No Japanese born on American territory has ever been proven guilty of sabotaging anything, and the 442 Regimental Combat Team (Japanese-Americans with mixed white and Nisei officers) proved to be the single most decorated unit in the Army. In several places they were sent in to relieve units such as the 82nd Airborne. Further, the use of Nisei interpreters in the Pacific War was obviously invaluable to the American effort. Despite the fact that these people were the best soldiers we had, their wives and children were obviously too dangerous to be allowed out on the street, and so they spent four years in America's first concentration camps—camps which, I note, are still available for potential use on recalcitrant blacks.

I don't pretend that the Indians were always chivalrous in their treatment of whites or of each other, and I fully realize that the concept of chivalry one finds in Bushido makes no mention of mercy to the helpless foe, but I maintain that we should do everything possible to redress our wrongs to these people before we claim to be holier than other nations on the score of racism and exploitation of minorities. None of the many Indians or Japanese I know aspires to be a Red or Brown WASP. What the Indians need is a school system which reinforces instead of disrupts their strong family system. The Japanese Americans have no need of economical aid—most of them make a lot more money than I do—but we should admit our government's GUILT (there is no other word) in the whole revolting incident and compensate these hard-working and honest people for the time they spent behind barbed wire. Also, we ought to purge the revolting stereotypes to which both races are subjected in our mass media. The ridiculous image which our movies give to Japanese and Japanese-Americans (generally played by Eurasian or Chinese actors) is ample cause for any number of anti-American riots in Tokyo universities.

That's about it, and thanks for reading this although I realize that you'll never print it.

Sincerely,
John Peter Koster
Hackensack, New Jersey

July 18, 1969

Dear Mr. Koster:

I am well aware of the fate that befell the American Indians, but I think you generalize too broadly when you say that this represents "the most shameful case study of brutality and greed ever recorded on the North American Continent."

I will not pretend to be an expert on Indian history, but I would refer you to one who is: Professor John Greenway, Professor of Anthropology at the University of Colorado. Professor Greenway contends that in recent years a great deal of nonsense has been written about the Indians and their suffering at the hands of the white man. The Indian, he says, has been idealized beyond recognition, and the policies of the European settlers, harsh though they were in many cases, such as the one you cite, were far from genocidal. Indeed, Greenway writes as follows:

"As for our treatment of the Indians, never in the entire history of the inevitable displacement of hunting tribes by advanced agriculturists in the 39,000 generations of mankind has a native people been treated with more consideration, decency and kindness. The Mongoloids in displacing the first comers of Asia, the Negroes in displacing the aborigines in Africa, and every other group following the biological law of the Competitive Exclusion Principle thought like the

131

Polynesian chief who once observed to a white officer:
'I don't understand you English. You come here and take our land then spend the rest of your lives trying to make up for it. When my people came to these islands, we just killed the inhabitants and that was the end of it.' "

Perhaps Professor Greenway is wrong, but the facts are perhaps more complicated than your statement would suggest. As you yourself recognize, many of the Indians were a savage and warlike people who massacred countless white settlers, frequently torturing them and horribly mutilating their bodies. They did not confine these practices to the whites, but behaved similarly toward other Indians. Professor Greenway points out that much of the money that the United States Government has paid to the Indians, for land which they claimed, has gone to tribes that were themselves invaders and usurpers of the land they occupied, having driven out, massacred or enslaved the previous owners.

In any case, I am not sure what the relevance of this is to the question of our questioning the morality of men who massacre and enslave their fellow citizens in the 20th century. Even if past history were all black with no rays of light, men could and should curse the continuing darkness and strive to bring about enlightenment.

I am afraid that your description of the Japanese relocation in World War II also suffers from some exaggeration. I would agree that the policy was unnecessary and unjust. I would not defend it, but it should not be painted as worse than it was for emotional effect. You should be aware of the fact that the only Japanese who were forced to relocate were those residing in California, Alaska and the western parts of Washington and Oregon. Those who lived in the other states and territories, including Hawaii, which had the greatest concentration of Japanese residents, were not

Koester: *"Our incarceration of the Nisei, or Japanese-Americans, is less gory (than our treatment of the Indians) but a great deal more stupid."*

Robertson: *"I would not defend (the policy) but it should not be painted as worse than it was for emotional effect . . . the government has paid out nearly $40 million to compensate those who claimed to have suffered losses as a result of the evacuation."*

Photo shows Japanese-Americans being moved to relocation centers during World War II.

COURTESY: WAR RELOCATION AUTHORITY

similarly treated. It is an exaggeration to say that the relatives of the Japanese soldiers were not allowed to walk the streets. The fact is that 110,000 were evacuated out of a total Japanese-American population of 285,000. Most of those who were evacuated and placed in camps were later permitted to leave if they could find jobs or a sponsor outside the camps. The result was that by the end of the war only 52,000 remained in the relocation centers. I understand that the government has paid out nearly $40 million to compensate those who claimed to have suffered losses as a result of the evacuation. The adequacy of the compensation may be questioned, but its payment reflects official recognition that an injustice was done.

I would like to reiterate a point I made in my letter to Marc Machiz. One of our serious problems is the willingness of people to exaggerate and distort the facts in order to prove a point. This misinforms, misleads and creates conflict and tension. Many talented writers have been guilty of this practice, and many of our newspapermen have forgotten the admonition of Herbert Bayard Swope, who said, "The first duty of the press is to be accurate. If it is accurate it follows that it will be fair." We badly need more writers who share Hemingway's belief that a "writer should be of as great probity and honesty as a priest of God." Of course, they also need to be willing to do the research necessary to get all the facts possible, which is frequently tiresome work.

Sincerely,

J. L. Robertson

Undated letter received in July 1969

Dear Sir:

Enclosed you will find one dollar which I would like you to give to the first person you see upon receiving it. Undoubtedly it will be the first time you will engage in unquestioning charity. If you need more money, please ask, and I will send as much as I can.

I don't own a car, but I do own a radio, but that Biafran student is welcome to it.

You see, sir, I and a number of my more dedicated friends are willing to live on stale bread and water if it serves as a solid object lesson for soulless America.

This is a "free" country—but there are pay toilets, transportation costs, and PRICES on essentials like food and medicine. Is it logical that in a "free" country, a man might be denied the essentials of his existence because he lacks the money? Welfare? Yes, it helps. And work? It's good for some. But how many of the hopelessly impoverished have you seen at the Federal Reserve? I have seen, met, and talked to many. Lent them money I knew they would never repay. I have cried with them and for them.

I hope you will recognize my concern. I can find no polite way to phrase this, but I hope you will accept this in the spirit it is meant: WAKE UP, Walk through the slums of your Washington.

"If you wish to gain perfect happiness, then sell all your goods, give the money to the poor, and come, follow Me."

W. T. Collete

Pawtuckett, Rhode Island

July 16, 1969

Dear Mr. Collette:

I appreciate your taking the time to write to me about your charitable activities. I admire your dedication to the cause of assisting the poor and downtrodden.

You should not jump to the conclusion that all those who do not follow your example are without charity. Nor should you assume that yours is the only way of helping people. You are perhaps familiar with the old saying that if you give a hungry man a fish, you provide him with food for one meal. If you give him fishing tackle and show him how to fish, you enable him to eat indefinitely.

Almsgiving ameliorates the suffering of the poor, but the only effective way to improve man's material well-being on a large scale is to increase his economic productivity. You must not denigrate the contribution made to human welfare by those who through their inventions, investments, managerial and organizational talent, etc., have made it possible for man to achieve a level of productivity many times greater than anything dreamed of prior to the Industrial Revolution. I do not know whether Henry Bessemer gave a great deal to charity or not, but I do know that he made a tremendous contribution to human welfare by discovering a way of producing high quality steel far more cheaply than it had ever been produced before. This helped make it possible to lay the rails for the railroads that opened up vast new territories for agricultural development, thus providing food in greater abundance. Would it have been better for Bessemer to have devoted his time and modest resources to almsgiving in London, or was it in the greater interest of mankind for him to struggle to invent and demonstrate the practicability of his process for making cheap steel? Is his contribution to be deplored because it resulted in his becoming personally very wealthy?

The fact is that this great advance in technology came about as early as it did only because Bessemer had accumulated enough capital through the exploitation of an earlier invention to finance his research into steel manufacture. The costly matter of building the plant to put his untried process into practical use was possible only because he and other men had accumulated enough capital to risk the investment. If they had avoided such accumulation and given all their income in excess of their personal needs to the poor, this step forward might never have been taken.

This is but one illustration of many that could be cited to show that the motivation of private gain and accumulation of personal wealth can contribute tremendously to general human welfare. What I want to emphasize is that the motivation is irrelevant in judging their actual contribution. It is not, however, irrelevant to consider what motivates men most effectively in deciding what kind of economic system we are going to have. We might prefer a world in which men were moved only by the most noble motives, but we must be realistic and recognize that many of our fellow human beings will work harder for their own material advantage than for altruistic reasons. If we want to harness the energies of these people and utilize their talents to promote the common welfare, we had best cater to what motivates them. We might wish that internal combustion engines would run on water, but we had better pour gasoline in the tanks if we want the automobiles to move.

You note that even though we call this a free country people must pay for nearly everything. "Free" has more than one meaning. This is a country where the citizens are relatively free from governmental compulsion in going about their daily activities. It would not be very free in this sense if the government forced the productive members of society to surrender all the fruits of their labors to the government for it to dispose of as it saw fit. This could properly be compared with slavery.

The free market system in which the transfer of goods and services is effected by matching the offers of buyers against the demands of sellers is an important element in our freedom. The market is free, in the sense that compulsion on buyers and sellers is largely absent, but the goods and services necessarily bear a cost. There are a few free goods in nature, such as fresh air, but this is only because the naturally created supply so greatly exceeds the demand that it is not necessary to devise a system of allocating the good. There is not an infinite supply of most goods and there is a

137

cost in their production and distribution. There must be a way of equalizing supply and demand, of determining how much of our scarce resources should be devoted to producing one thing rather than another. There must be a way of placing exchange value on the goods that men want to exchange so that the producers and sellers are satisfied that their efforts have been adequately rewarded and so the buyers can make a rational choice between the alternative uses of their purchasing power. This is what prices are all about. Do not assume that you can dispense with the price system without first studying both the theory and the practice. The countries that have tried to improve on the free market by substituting government decrees as a means of setting prices have encountered horrendous problems. One consequence has frequently been the discouragement of production of needed goods and production of other goods in excess of what the consumers want. This results in tremendous waste, and even though the intentions be good, the effect on human welfare is negative.

I thank you for your well-intended offer of money to assist me in my own charitable activities. I am sorry that you were so uncharitable as to judge my character harshly without ever having met me. You have offered me a passage from the New Testament, and I will offer one to you. Jesus also said, "Judge not that ye be not judged."

I am returning the dollar bill which you enclosed. I am sure that you can find good use for it in your admirable charitable work. I wish you success in all your endeavors, and I hope that in the course of your studies you will not miss the opportunity to learn more about the science of economics, which is the study of how to achieve equitable distribution of goods and services while maximizing their production and increasing the general well-being of mankind.

Sincerely,

J. L. Robertson

Dear Sir,

I believe that the letter by Marc Machiz was an attempt at constructive criticism and not a pessimistic rejection of American society, and I am sure that this was his own intention. On the basis of this contention I must of necessity come to his and society's defense.

I realize that you have a much broader base of knowledge and experience from which to draw information, but I also believe that this young man is expressing his ideals because of his avid interest in his own country and in the world.

Our forefathers doubtless had the best intentions in the world when they sought a country in which all the basic individual rights of man could be realized. Marc is most probably speaking of the period of his own lifetime when he says that we are trending more and more toward materialism, and only he can relate with authority the evidence observed within his specific environment and not from a nebulous past before his lifetime and in the future. Few elect to emigrate from the U.S. because of pragmatic reasons including the right to live in any manner one wishes as long as this does not have a harmful effect on any other individual or on society as a whole, and because if one observes certain shortcomings, he may speak freely of them in an attempt at improvement.

The state does enjoy the right of eminent domain and saw fit to seize all lands from the Indian and relegate him to reservations. This native American, who could adapt to and live with the forces of nature without any way destroying or contaminating it, has never received any just compensation for the taking away of his life ways and livelihood.

I think we have to judge the "peoples' park" in Berkeley on the basis of the end, and the means to accomplish that end, resulting in an observable and outstanding addition to the community. Weren't these students a part of that great institution that could not find a peaceable solution to this minor controversy?

No people in the world are as generous in the giving of money as the American people, and many of them do not resent the increasing tax burden that goes in part to help support the more unfortunate in our own country and abroad. Might this not be explained by the fact that it is much easier to give away a nominal sum than to get involved personally in helping someone help themselves?

The example of the Egyptian banker wishing to attract foreign capital does not hardly reflect the desires of Latin Americans. The actions of Peru in seizing American oil interests and the Chilean nationalizing of Anaconda's mines plus the anti-U.S. demonstrations in the countries recently visited by Governor Rockefeller of New York would be more valid for the manifestation of the true thoughts and feelings of the Latin American nations. And if our altruism is such a virtue, why have only two to three percent of American profits from our interests in these countries been reinvested in these foreign markets and the rest repatriated? American companies' wages have helped raise living standards for those "lucky" few who work for them, but what does it do to the standards of the remaining populace?

Former Secretary of Health, Education and Welfare John Gardner was perceptive enough to realize that, though we have the most stable and democratic government in the world, it still does not possess the flexibility required to change rapidly enough with this ever-growing and changing world. Good intentions are usually sought, but it is important to realize that they do not always result in the greatest benefit for the largest number, and also it is this result which will be analyzed and not the original gesture. Our American legal system as well as science and history are based on a precept of this sort. A proud heritage and a just government will never interfere with the attitudes of an individual and his endeavoring to seek what is best for himself and his culture. It is left to a man to try to advance through life in the direction of his inner feelings and desires, for only then will he ever meet with real success.

Respectfully,
Sp4 Charles R. Russell
San Francisco, California

July 28, 1969

Dear Mr. Russell:

The many letters I have received since my letter to Marc Machiz was published have included several which like yours have touched on factual issues that I dealt with in a critical way.

As I indicated in my letter to Marc, we can reduce tension and conflict if we can reach agreement on our facts. Let me discuss a few points in your letter with respect to which the information available to me differs from that which you accept as true.

1. You state that the American Indian has never received just compensation for having been deprived of his way of life and livelihood. You may not be aware of the fact that the U.S. Government has paid very large sums of money to the various Indian tribes to compensate them for the loss of their lands. After World War II Congress established the Indian Claims Commission to consider the claims made by Indians that the initial compensation paid under the treaties negotiated in the 18th and 19th centuries was inadequate. This commission has studied the claims and endeavored to appraise the value of the Indian lands at the time of their transfer. They have recommended that additional payments totaling $305 million be paid. It is estimated that the total amounts paid for the land covered by these claims would be in the vicinity of $370 million.

In considering these figures, bear in mind that Thomas Jefferson purchased the entire Louisiana Territory from France for what was considered to be the large sum of $15 million. I am sure we have paid the Indians occupying land covered by the Louisiana Purchase many times that amount for their claims.

You may not regard the compensation that has been paid as just, but let us not obscure the fact that large sums of money have been paid. I think that before the layman decides whether these payments are just or not he should probe as deeply into the matter as have the members of the Indian Claims Commission and the judges that have considered all the facts at their disposal before making the awards.

2. You state the so-called "People's Park" in Berkeley resulted in an observable and outstanding addition to the community. According to reports that I have seen, the "park" was considered by the residents in the immediate area to be an eyesore and a public nuisance. It seems clear from the demands that were made by those responsible for squatting on this land that they had no desire to negotiate a peaceable solution, and they ignored invitations to negotiate.

3. You suggest that the action of the Government of Peru in expropriating the holdings of the International Petroleum Corp. is indicative of the attitude of all Latin America toward foreign investment. The fact is that even while it was expropriating IPC property the Peruvian Government was assuring the world that it wanted and welcomed foreign investment. The IPC case, it has insisted, was exceptional for historical reasons. I would not, of course, contend that no one in Latin America is critical of foreign investment. The attitude of the Egyptian banker I cited is not representative of all the people of Egypt, much less Latin America. What I would emphasize is that even in a country that has been as hostile to foreign investment as the United Arab Republic,

142

there is a sign of a change in sentiment as a result of the learning that comes from experience. The dominant line of thought in Latin America is favorable to foreign private investment. There are those who would like to give a contrary impression and drive out foreign capital even if it means causing serious damage to the economies of their own countries. I would suggest that the mobs that demonstrated against Governor Rockefeller included a high percentage of people of this type. I would not conclude that they were representative of either the masses or the best brains in their countries.

4. You state that only 2 or 3 per cent of the profits of American firms investing in Latin American countries have been reinvested. According to data published in the "Survey of Current Business" of October 1968, 24 per cent of the earnings of American firms in Latin America were reinvested in that area in 1966. This percentage fell to 14 per cent in 1967. In general, firms will tend to reinvest part of their profits abroad as long as the climate for investment is encouraging and the prospects are promising. Unfortunately, incidents such as the expropriation of the IPC properties in Peru can put a serious damper on investment in not only the country doing the expropriating, but in neighboring countries as well. Investors are not motivated by altruism, but by the lure of attractive financial rewards. It does little good to appeal to their sympathy to induce them to put funds into situations where there is serious danger that they will lose their capital. That does not mean that the results of their investments will not be beneficial to large numbers of people. It is incorrect to assume that the benefits accrue only to those directly employed by the foreign businesses. The expenditures for supplies, services and salaries are respent by the recipients, giving rise to additional income. If you have ever visited a ghost town you will see the evidence of the many different types of economic activity that were once dependent upon the em-

ployment generated by a single mine.

I hope that these observations will be of value in demonstrating how factual information or its lack can help shape value judgments.

Sincerely,

J. L. Robertson

July 2, 1969

Dear Mr. Robertson:

May I say that I agree with everything you said about preserving and protecting all the things we hold dear in our country? However, one aspect of our country bothers me so I am writing you about your omission of it.

It is what our nation says it is for self-determination in South Vietnam where our boys are fighting. At the same time our actions in recognizing all dictator nations except Russia and China as friends and neighbors. They are Greece, Portugal, Spain, and practically all of Central and South America. Why is this? I have been unable to get an answer from either the Johnson or Nixon Administrations. I hope to get a sensible answer from you but I may not.

Is it to protect our large foreign investments or is it due to our unreasonable fear of Communism?

Since actions are louder than words I fear that our government is not telling us the real reason why we are fighting in South Vietnam. I am not a Red. I am a veteran of World War I.

No one can tell me of the fear of dictators in Spain and Portugal. I saw it in both countries on a visit in 1967. There was no self-determination in either country and those who raised their voices for freedom are given long prison sentences. To class them as our friends is really ridiculous and does us no good in world affairs.

What do you say?

Sincerely,

Everett H. Wallace

Milwaukee, Wisconsin

Dear Mr. Wallace: July 17, 1969

I know that the question you raise about our friendship with countries that are ruled by dictators is one that troubles many people, and I am sorry that you have not been able to obtain an answer to it from those who are far better qualified to reply than I am. Obviously, I cannot give you an official explanation, but I will proffer my own personal view for whatever it is worth.

It is quite evident that our form of democratic government frequently does not thrive and prosper in countries whose populations are characterized by high illiteracy and mass poverty. I am not sure that it is either the illiteracy or the poverty that is inimical to democratic forms. It may be other factors that underlie and contribute to both the illiteracy and poverty. Edmund Burke once said, "Kings will be tyrants from policy when subjects are rebels from principle." There may be elements in the character of some peoples that make orderly government very difficult except with a high degree of authoritarianism.

The degree of authoritarianism can vary widely. I do not believe that we have any right to insist that every country in the world maintain a government that is no more authoritarian than ours. If we established that as the determinant of diplomatic recognition, we could greatly economize on our diplomatic missions abroad.

It appears clear to me that our tendency to "accept" some authoritarian regimes and to look with disfavor on others is related to two factors. One is the degree of authoritarianism that prevails. It seems to me that there is a sharp division between a government that is merely authoritarian and one that is totalitarian. The latter endeavors to control every phase of economic, political, and social activity in the country. Its power is so oppressive that it would lose a very substantial part of the population if it permitted free emigration, as was the case in East Germany before the wall sealed

145

off the exit routes. One of the easily identifiable characteristics of a completely totalitarian regime is that it does not permit free emigration.

I believe that we are justified in looking with some disfavor on any regime that is so oppressive that it offers death as the only escape to those who find life in the country intolerable.

You will agree, I believe, that the countries that you enumerated in your letter—Greece, Spain, Portugal, and many of the Latin American countries—do not fall in this category. These countries place restrictions on political activity and speech and press that are more restrictive than we would tolerate, but they allow considerable freedom in the economic, social, and religious spheres. Conditions may be oppressive for many of their citizens, but they do not apparently have to fear the kind of population hemorrhage that hit East Germany before the wall was built. Indeed, Greece and Spain encourage people to go to other European countries to work.

However, even extreme totalitarianism **per se** does not explain our coolness toward certain regimes. I think we can distinguish between tyrannies that are distasteful but not dangerous and those that are both distasteful and dangerous because of their aggressive designs. We do not admire the regime in Haiti, but we obviously have nothing to fear from it. We do have something to fear from Mr. Castro in Cuba, since he has been actively engaged in endeavoring to subvert governments throughout Latin America and fasten his form of totalitarianism upon them. Moreover, he has been active in inciting subversion in our country and has permitted, in the past, installation of offensive nuclear missiles directed against our cities.

Both you and I probably have neighbors with whom we may differ on religious, political, or other grounds. If we can count on them to come to our aid, say when our homes are invaded by a burglar, we may look upon them as friends to whom we may extend courtesies and assistance in time of need. At least, they will be better friends than burglars.

Sincerely,

J. L. Robertson

July 7, 1969

Dear Mr. Robertson:

Having read your reply to Mr. Machiz' statements and being an old man interested in social problems all my life, that is my adult life, I cannot resist the temptation to comment to you on your letter, and must add, with no hopes or illusions that they will be taken seriously by you. You question Mr. Machiz' statement that "American society has always been materialistic." May I ask why man moved from the "stone ax" (Secretary McNamara) to the automatic machine unless it was his material needs that forced him to do so? His "spiritual" life had nothing to do with it and the advantages he has taken of his fellow man don't indicate "spiritual" behavior. We have an example in our own country, the use that was made of the chattel slave which you mention. The chattel slave wasn't freed because man was sorry for him, his treatment since he was freed proves my point.

The chattel slave was freed because he was in the way of progress. If capitalism was going to make its contribution to progress by solving the problem of production, which it has amply done (today the modern tools of production are efficient enough to produce enough for everyone everywhere in the world) it had to have a free and educated working class educated so they could continually improve the efficiency of the machines of production to meet competition in home and world markets, and free to be hired or fired as the home and world markets could absorb the products of the efficient machine. There was nothing spiritual about it. It was strictly

147

a "material" proposition. Also you are stretching your imagination when you imply it was for spiritual reasons this country was settled. They came here because land could be had almost for the asking and as Gifford Pinchot, the noted conservationist, said long ago, "Without the ownership of property and natural resources, prosperity (and may I add security) is out of reach."

Also your statement that "World War one and two were fought to resist authoritarian and totalitarian movements" doesn't hold up. General Hugh Johnson speaking to "World Peace Ways" in 1935 said: "There never was a war at arms that was not merely the extension of a preceding war of commerce grown fiercer until the weapons of war seemed no longer sufficiently deadly." President Eisenhower speaking to the Governors Council in 1956 said this about Vietnam. This country had then spent two hundred and fifty million dollars there. "So when this country votes money to help that war we are voting for the cheapest way to get the tin and tungsten we so greatly value from that area."

General David Shoup, (former) Marine Corps Commandant, was asked by Representative Wm. F. Ryan in these words: "I take it you don't buy the argument the vital interest of the U.S. is at stake in Vietnam." General Shoup replied: "I do not. I have never seen a timetable of what would be the detriment to our national interest if we had not done anything but send a bunch of advisers in there. . . . They just try to keep the people worried about the communists crawling up the banks of Pearl Harbor or crawling up the beaches of Los Angeles which of course is a bunch of unadulterated poppycock."

Senator Gore of Tennessee (Congressional Record March 20, 1969) said this: "Of course we would like to see a democratic republic in South Vietnam, the more in our own image the more to our liking. But this is a matter of ideological preference **not for our security**. Whether there is one

148

Vietnam or two, whether the government of either or both be democratic or autocratic or communist no genuine threat to our security is involved."

The above should be enough evidence to prove that wars are not fought for ideological or political reasons as you imply in your letter.

On economics I hold with Gustavius Myers when he says in his book "The History of the Great American Fortunes": "Surveying historical events in a large way, however, it is not to be regretted that capitalism had its own unbridaled way and its growth was not checked. Its development to the unbearable maximum had to come in order to prepare a ripe way for a newer stage in civilization. He (the capitalist) fitted as an appropriate a part in his day as the predatory barron in feudal times."

On the spiritual side of life I hold with Sir Arthur Bryant in his book "The Age of Chivalry" when he said: "Yet though the church existed to teach men how to live justly, it was all too apparent that this was what so many of its ministers failed to do themselves. It was not, as the saints sought to make it, above the world; it was part of the world itself. Since every world activity conducted in Christ's name and with the Church's blessing, it followed that Christianity had become a very worldly religion. The richer society grew and the more men laid up for themselves treasures upon earth, the more materially minded grew the Church." "Of all the ways of Christians to make war seem holy, the simplest way is to get Jesus into it. (Reverend Harry Fosdick) The above should prove that the minority among us, the owning class are "concerned with the accumulation of material wealth."

A society, best described by one of its staunchest upholders, namely Franklin D. Roosevelt, in these words: "The mechanical (meaning the tools of production) has brought about a class division of humanity into classes where less than one in a hundred owned and controlled the very lives and fortunes of the other ninety-nine" can't hope to last forever in an age of reason. And add to that the "ninety-nine" do the world's work. As Bishop Vincent Sheen (sic) said long ago: "There are but two classes—one class owns and the other class manages and produces." If this letter has not reached your waste basket long before this, I will close with a

Yours truly,
R. V. Brandborg
Little Falls, Minnesota

July 17, 1969

Dear Mr. Brandborg:

I hope it is apparent to you that I do not accept the materialistic determinism of Karl Marx. One does not prove that all human actions are rooted in materialistic motivations merely by stating that to be the case. The test of this interpretive tool should lie in its predictive ability, not in one's ability to find some materialistic motivation for events that have already occurred. The Marxists have proven to be the world's worst prophets, but this has never been permitted to shatter their faith in their interpretive devices. They are experts at telling us why things happened as they did, but why we should place any credence in their explanation is not at all clear.

I hope that you will take the time to read Djilas' new book, "The Unperfect Society." I think you will find it interesting and stimulating.

Sincerely,
J. L. Robertson

part 7

are we communicating?

A few people have said that I was wasting my time in trying to deal with the questions raised by my correspondents in a substantive way. They have been pessimistic about the possibility of opening lines of communication with the younger generation in this way. They argue that the youngsters do not read and will not listen.

That may be true of some. But it obviously is not true of those who wrote to me. I had the feeling in almost every case that my young correspondents were sincere seekers after truth. I do not know what impact my letters had on all of them. However, I did receive one letter that made me feel richly rewarded for the time that I had devoted to his correspondence. It was from Marc Machiz, the student who had gotten the snowball rolling in the first place. Here is what he said:

"July 3, 1969

"Dear Mr. Robertson:

"It was a great honor for me to have a letter of mine published along with one written by a man of your great ability and prominence. Even more importantly I want to thank you for taking the time to reply to me so completely. It is gratifying

151

to know that a man in your position is as deeply concerned with the solution of our social problems as you are.

"As you pointed out in your letter, property rights are one component in the spectrum of human rights, not separate and distinct. Regrettably, I overlooked this in my letter. Perhaps the answer to the problems of the United States lies, in part, in striking the proper balance between all of the various human rights including the right to property. If so, it is encouraging to me that there are men of your ability and awareness who attempt to strike that balance.

"Respectfully yours,
Marc Machiz"

Communication is possible. Perhaps it is easier with other people's children (or with other children's parents) than with one's own in many cases. One of my correspondents was a mother in New Holland, Pennsylvania, who sent me copies of an exchange of letters she had had with a young student. She had heard him speak and had been impressed with his intelligence but had never met him. She took it upon herself to open up some channels of communication with him. The letters she sent me are, I think, good illustrations of a dialogue between the generations that may be fruitful. I am including them here, slightly edited to remove personal references that would not be of general interest, as an illustration of the communication that is actually taking place.

July 25, 1969

Dear Mr. Robertson:

Just yesterday I happened to see and read the exchange of letters between you and Marc Machiz. It was thrilling to read your reply to Machiz' letter because you said things I have tried so often to say, so much better and so much more convincingly. I think you spoke eloquently for many, many of our generation.

Earlier this week, on July 22, **before** I read your letter, I tried to reply to a similar challenge. The parallel of the ques-

152

tions both you and I received, the answers I tried to write and the outstanding achievement of your reply was so striking that I am sending you a copy of the exchange of letters I had with Rusty Cox.

Like you, I never met the young man to whom I replied, but we have a daughter who attends Gettysburg College where he is also a student. I heard him on a panel of students at Gettysburg this spring speaking very articulately and logically about raising the scholastic standards of Gettysburg College. He did such a fine job as compared to the other students who spoke poorly and clamored for the "power" they wanted that I wrote him a note commending him. He wrote back a beautifully composed letter, thanked me for being interested, and asked if I wouldn't continue to write him about the problems of his generation. This was his third letter.

Again, the parallel of the thoughts was most interesting to me and I thought it might also be interesting to you and to David Lawrence who is also receiving a copy and whose thoughts on paper I so often admire.

Thank you, Mr. Robertson, for expressing so well your thoughts and ideas which need to be expounded much more profusely to our young people today.

Sincerely,
Marian L. Mosser
New Holland, Pennsylvania

July 7, 1969

Dear Mrs. Mosser:

Down here we hear nothing of the news from the East, so you will have to inform me of the most recent developments in the war against The Establishment.

I would like to give you some food for thought. I am not necessarily in agreement with this, but it may get the old wheels turning again in our attempt to understand my gener-

153

ation and its problems. In the July issue of "Playboy," Rod Steiger was interviewed. I would like to quote him in a few places.

"I want to continue to do movies for people who are looking for new beliefs, movies for people who have said to their parents, 'Sorry folks, but I think you blew it and I don't want to go your way.'"

"Young people are now awakening older people to the fact that there is beauty in everybody. They're looking more deeply into things. The youth of this country is quite rightly saying, 'This is a one-time trip and I don't want to wear these masks any more.'"

"Before every new era, there has to be a catalytic period of chaos and struggle. These kids reflect the nation's disenchantment with the old answers and the old ways. The hypocrisy has been exposed. A man teaches his child to be honest. He says his boss is a schmuck, and then his child walks in and there's the boss sitting at the table for dinner with the father falling all over him, running to get drinks. Older people have sacrificed themselves for creature comforts. The top societies of the world have everything, yet they're surrounded by misery. The kids are discovering that Daddy and Mommy and government and religion don't have the integrity they were taught to believe in. Organized religion is a disease, and governments aren't really functioning. They are both despicable because they promise things they never deliver."

Mr. Steiger is 44. He is no authority, only a celebrity. He has an opinion, which he may expound. We listen and consider. We need not agree.

Before I close, let me raise one more point. I am told that isolationism is a poor policy for the U.S.A. We cannot sit back and let Vietnam be taken over by Russia. We assert our power in all parts of the world, lest we find our power dwindling. Thousands upon thousands of Americans starve annually. Thousands more die of cancer. Millions are illiterate. Millions are on relief. America is torn from within. Ghettos and slums multiply. Highways crumble. Crops die. Riots continue. Traffic deaths mount. Hospitals are over-crowded. Nevertheless, we must look beyond our own suffer-ing to the other side of the world. While our countrymen starve, our youth is sent abroad. A young man cannot go to college for he must help support his family. He is drafted, his family goes hungry. He is killed.

But who am I to question the decisions of those herring-boned, pin-striped, club-tied, wing-tipped, cigar-smoking, Cadillac-driving legislators who return home to their air-con-ditioned houses after a hard day on the Hill. They have gone to law school. They read three newspapers every morning. They are aware of our needs. The poor and sick cry out, yet the affluent turn their heads away. We must not limit our-selves. We must reach out. We must remain in Vietnam, in Berlin, in Laos. We must never resort to isolationism.

This month we land on the moon!

Sincerely,
Rusty Cox
Houston, Texas

July 22, 1969

Dear Rusty,

There is no day I have felt equal to a rebuttal of the chal-lenge you've given, but perhaps these historic days of moon exploration are as good as any, at least to start. American ingenuity has not yet brought the "Columbia" back to earth at this point in time, but we have every hope that this, too, will be accomplished with flawless perfection.

Just moments ago I heard David Brinkley commenting

that now that we have gone to the moon there is a tendency to believe we can do anything, but that this is not true. (I believe it is true technologically and scientifically.) He pointed out that the achievement was made because everyone worked toward this agreed goal, but that if you said, for instance, now go ahead and clear the slums, immediately there would be 100 reasons and 100 questions to keep man from this goal— i.e., how do you keep an area from becoming again a slum after it has been cleared?

Maybe you don't think, as Bertrand Russell does not, that we had any business going to the moon, but it seems to me man had to do this, that it is an innate part of the minds which God created to drive them farther and farther to the depths of knowledge, understanding and truth. There should be no "last frontier."

That the accomplishment was finally made by Americans is as it should be—for where else on this earth are there free men to rise to the challenge of the impossible but here? It was proved by late entry into both World War I and World War II—lagging far behind in equipment and trained men, they pulled together to defeat an insidious aggressor.

You have probably received some of the reading material I've sent your way. It was meant to give you some different points of view for you to consider. It's like feeding a computer, perhaps, and the more background information you absorb, the better able you will be to find an answer to your questions.

Putting my thoughts on paper is difficult in tying them into your letter, but let's make an attempt. . . .

You mentioned "the war against the Establishment" and Rod Steiger's remarks about youth today saying to their parents that they "blew it" and they don't want to go the same way. Aside from the argument of whether or not it was right for us to go to the moon, no one can deny it was a supreme accomplishment and it looks to me like it was the

Establishment—the "hypocritical parents" of today's rest-
less youth—who made this unbelievable accomplishment.
The minds which conquered seemingly unsurmountable
problems belong to men who even came from the same college campuses which your generation belittles. The industry
and ingenuity behind these accomplishments seem much too
huge for us to grasp, but it was done nevertheless.

These men are the breed of people who Steiger says have
"sacrificed themselves for creature comforts." We must remember, both you and I, not to say **all** or **everybody** about
anything or any people. To say "the Establishment" is all
wrong and should be abolished because they have not solved
our problems, you would have to, as Leo Rosten says in some
of the material sent you, "by the same reasoning . . . blow
up all hospitals (and perhaps execute all doctors, biologists
and researchers): they have not abolished disease."

Many of these "all wrong people" have sacrificed much
of themselves to give you and your peers today the opportunities they did not have, nor does the youth of any other nation
in the world. They are not all of them consumed with social
climbing and materialism, but continue to plug away trying
to do their level best to advance mankind in innumerable
ways, just as the men at Baylor I'm sure are doing. From all
of the struggles they have known, they have gained **practical**
knowledge and **experience,** something the untried do not yet
have. They have learned answers as well as questions. They
have defined goals, they have to think fast and logically; they
have to work hard; they have accomplished all there is for
you to see as you look around Houston or any other area in the
United States.

Wherever you are and wherever you look, you can see
both the good and the bad. I do not think it is a new thing, or
that "young people are now awakening older people to the
fact that there is beauty in everybody." Wasn't that taught
about 2,000 years ago by a man who had little education and

traveled but a few miles from home, and haven't people been writing about it ever since?

The things that your generation cry are wrong with the world are not new. Most probably in some form, they are all as old as life, but we continue to try to correct what is wrong, knowing full well we can never reach perfection. Let me hasten to assure you I am not defending the things that are wrong; I agree they exist, that for many people their ruler (either meaning) is materialism; I am not defending legislators for the political mire they deal us; I am not even defending Vietnam, because I'm still not sure about Vietnam. What I do feel about Vietnam is that if we were going in there in the first place, we should have done it on the basis of winning a war and finishing it in very short order.

I am defending the basic structure of this nation, the foundations which have contributed to its greatness, with no equal anywhere. I am defending capitalism and the capitalists themselves. I am firmly convinced that no goverment, no political structure, no union, no social society, no church, no missionaries, no welfare, no educational institution, no do-gooders anywhere have done for the people of this nation (and also drew people from nations all over the world) what American industry—and capitalism—has done.

We will never, never raise the "minority"—be they black, white, blue or orange—out of their "misery" by giving them more and more money for less and less work because, I think, (1) God did **not** create all of us equal (and He must have had a good reason), (2) they don't want to be helped to change, or to work and produce like the rest of us are required to do. The day they learn to pull themselves up by their own bootstraps, as many of them have already done, and have the desire to earn their own way, encouraged and helped by the rest of us, the problems will disappear.

We spoke recently to a West Virginia University senior who did student teaching in a small West Virginia school where there were third generation reliefers. I asked him if he felt sorry for them and he said, "No—there's work there for them to do, but this is a way of life for them." You can add that to a large percentage of other such experiences.

There was another incident this summer at Williamsburg when at the end of a tour of the Capitol a visitor remarked that we have a great deal to be thankful for to these early Americans, an articulate guide said, "I must tell you about a young man I know who attended William and Mary College. He was a junior there and a member of the R.O.T.C. He decided to join the Marines and before he left he was talking to some of his classmates who were protestors, campus radicals and the like. He told them he felt it was a privilege for him to go to Vietnam to help defend the right they had to be dissenters. He never came back from Vietnam. He was killed there last July. He was no very special or extraordinary student, just a very regular guy. He happened to be my son—and I just felt I had to tell you this."

A friend of mine here at New Holland said in discussing the generation battle:

"Now, there's the question of government. Younger folks want to change things, right? Well, how many youngsters are running for office? Seems to me they get all caught up in politics trying to help some established politicians get elected. Are they afraid to try on their own? Sure, there are age restrictions in politics, but not on the local level. Why don't they battle the local machines where corruption **really** gets its start, and where they can really get things accomplished?

"You know what I think? I think they are afraid to dive into a pitched battle with experienced people on a toe-to-toe basis. Get a couple of these kids alone and they dwell on the three-button suit argument. They are anti-establishment, whatever the hell that means.

I read of the 23-year-old kid who borrowed $800 and is now worth $5 million. Is he part of the establishment they are against? If so, I guess I can only assume they are not anti-establishment as much as they are anti-initiative. And therein lies, I believe, the problem. . . .

"Did these kids initiate the rebirth of Philadelphia? Or was it men who took a look at what was going on and decided it was time to throw out a gang of entrenched politicians who had been bleeding the city dry? It took men of experience, vision and courage to do the job.

"America was moving on its own natural juices before the Kennedy brothers stirred the pot. I was at Little Rock when Ike sent us to open Central High to Negroes. Was America moving then? And today I drive hundreds of miles on highways that older men of vision saw necessary and started to build.

"I have faith in America and I am sure we would have moved steadily ahead and cities would have improved, and the people would have overcome the crime problem and education would have moved ahead WITHOUT the prodding of unkempt, universally ugly riff-raff who were goading police at the President's inauguration, shouting 'pig' at every policeman they saw, and rattling the sabres of revolution in the cities and campuses.

"Yes, there is a lot to be done and it is good that young people are interested. But they had better learn one thing right now. You can't change a country like this through revolution. The decision-makers that are here today are going to stay in power until the majority of Americans are convinced they are wrong. And bearded, dirty bands of Leftists aren't going to get the job done. It's the men who have initiative, clear, logical minds, patient men who know how to work diligently toward a goal who are going to shape the future of the country."

The author is not of the "older generation." He's several years younger than Neil Armstrong. Like he, I am thankful you and your generation are concerned and interested. I am certain if you watch and wait and listen and learn, you and your generation are going to accomplish much. Right at the moment, without the practical knowledge and experience, it would be somewhat like a little girl saying, "Let me bake that cake, Mother," but when she begins the task, she learns that it is not nearly so simple as it looks from a distance and realizes why even with the "practical knowledge and experience" a Mother can sometimes even ruin a packaged cake mix!

Mary Lee brought home a good thought from one of the speakers you had at Gettysburg last Fall. She related that he said he wouldn't want to be operated on by a surgeon who went to a medical college where he and the other students decided what they were going to study. Granted students are taught much in schools and colleges which is totally irrelevant and unnecessary and from teachers and professors who do not belong even near a campus, but maybe this is part of life and realizing we will not find perfection anywhere, we learn to separate the wheat from the chaff, and sift out for ourselves what will teach us the most and help us on our way.

Near the end of your letter you've made some pretty strong statements. We agreed we need not agree to discuss and I would certainly take issue with the idea that we are asserting our power in Vietnam so that it does not dwindle. Do you recall any other nation who won the wars we've fought who then helped the defeated nation to become again self-sustaining instead of building her own empire with the conquered nations? "Thousands upon thousands of Americans starve annually"—if they do (and I doubt this), it's because they do not use the money they have, earned or otherwise, to buy the right kind of food instead of what they do spend it for. "Millions are illiterate"—why? "Millions are on relief"— why? "America is torn from within"—they were united this weekend and if it is torn from within, let's assume it's because there are planned and planted people to deliberately incite division. "Ghettos and slums multiply"—then where has all the effort and money gone, and why have I seen so much "urban renewal" and slum clearance? And so on. I think it would be pretty difficult to justify the broad, sweeping statement that our people starve while our youth is sent abroad and that the families of those who do not return go hungry. We do not turn our heads or our hearts away from people who are truly in need. Not one of us would deny aid to those who cannot really help themselves. Countless millions of us go to work to fight poverty.

This has been far too long, Rusty, and I know I have not answered all of your questions; and I know that even though I have struggled, I have not found all of the right words. I am grateful to you for your willingness to listen to this older generation and perhaps we'll have an opportunity to discuss it verbally at Gettysburg some day. I am just as interested in your thoughts and open to your discussions. How else can we both learn, one from another?

Sincerely,
Marian Mosser
New Holland, Pennsylvania

Another correspondent, Mr. Craig Brown of Ft. Thomas, Kentucky, raised an interesting question about the method of communicating. He suggested the desirability of utilizing a more effective approach than straight confrontation of opposing points of view, and discussed a technique that he thought was more effective. In replying I described my own view of how the mature human mind tends to reject certain information and ideas because of its built-in filter. This is what makes communication between parent and child difficult at times, and I discuss in my reply to Mr. Brown some suggestions on how this may be overcome.

July 7, 1969

Dear Mr. Robertson:

Your rebuttal of Marc Machiz was logical, well thought, well written and complete in every sense. I might add that I agree vehemently with every word in your text.

And now comes the inevitable, "However."

In spite of your painstaking logic and understanding, I'm sure that deep inside, you know that everything you said was lost on that young man and all the others who have taken his side. The reason is due to a vague thing which I shall call "the phenomenon of confrontation." It's really not a phenomenon. It simply relates to the truism that when one takes a definite position, it forces someone else to either surrender or to erect a defense. In either case, there emerges either hostility or submission. Out of this chaos, communication and cooperation vanish.

I do not agree with our young friend's logic, while yours is brilliant in its clarity. But isn't that because I was on your side before the battle began? The best you can hope to gain is the obedience of a beaten person, not the cooperation of an ally. What to do about it? I don't know for sure, but I think the key words would be "cooperation," "inquiry," "wonderment" and "discovery." My partner, Sam Beall, who is older and wiser than I, often reminds me that when self-importance marches through the door, free inquiry flies out the window.

For some time my partner and I have been writing films for industry that instead of commanding obedience, invite the cooperation of an audience. It is the beckoning finger as opposed to the pounding fist. We have noticed that where a confrontation of facts will fail, the process of free inquiry will triumph.

You and I would both like to change the attitude of the Marc Machiz's of our society. We would like their intellects to be turned to the positive aspects of our culture. Many of these people will discover reasons to change, such as actually living your analogy of the $500 used car. But you may agree that this is slow and painful, and possibly may never happen. Mr. Beall and I, in the films we write, like to modify attitudes by taking no position against which someone can build a defense. This, we believe, is essential to building a communication as opposed to merely transmitting. We simply tell an interesting story, preferably a fictitious one. Thus we set the stage for the audience to discover for themselves reasons to change an attitude, follow a plan or buy a product.

In the case of those whose attitude is that our system of free enterprise must be torn down, things may have gone too far to employ our stage for discovery. Still, the answer must lie somewhere short of waiting and hoping for these young people to grow up and discover, while rooting through the ashes of their lives, that perhaps they had been operating on a false premise.

Apparently you cared enough to write a thoughtful letter to the young student. It just may be that some combined thought would produce a vehicle that encourages an easier form of discovery of some of the reasons why you and I care to preserve our way of life.

Please let me know if my letter has kindled a spark.

Sincerely yours,
Craig M. Brown
Ft. Thomas, Kentucky

Dear Mr. Brown:

Thank you for your interesting letter of July 7. I agree with you that confrontation and debate seldom change the minds of the antagonists, but that does not mean that it is a waste of time. I felt that it was worth the effort to reply to Marc Machiz' letter, and the effort has been rewarded. I have received a very nice letter from Marc, in which he says:

"As you pointed out in your letter, property rights are one component in the spectrum of human rights, not separate and distinct. Regrettably, I overlooked this in my letter. Perhaps the answer to the problems of the United States lies, in part, in striking the proper balance between all of the various human rights including the right to property."

I have received many letters from others who read the exchange, but none gave me as much satisfaction as this one, which indicated that perhaps I had helped an obviously talented and idealistic young man achieve a broader philosophic perspective.

Undoubtedly, there is greater possibility of influencing the thinking of young people than people of mature years. These youngsters are having their ideas molded by a variety of influences. The rebellion against what they have been taught by their parents is not spontaneous. It reflects a clash of ideas, with the new and unconventional ideas frequently winning out.

The reason these ideas triumph in some cases seems to be because the young people, as their contacts and inquiries broaden, become convinced that many of the things they were taught as children are not true. This may be because they encounter teachers who seem to be more knowledgeable than their own parents who provide them with information that undermines their beliefs, or at least calls them into question. If they have been taught, for example, that George Washington had no faults and they encounter a teacher who is able to demonstrate that he had some human frailties, they may then jump to the conclusion that those who gave them the impression that Washington was perfect cannot be relied upon as sources of information. They may be inclined to look to the debunker as a more trustworthy guide.

At this stage in a person's life, what one believes is very closely related to whom one believes.

It seems to me that it is necessary to expose the unreliability of those sources of information that are indeed unreliable. Lies and distortions cannot be expected to fall of their own accord. They must be refuted. In refuting them, one automatically reduces the influence of those who have been responsible for them.

It is, of course, much easier to expose individual inaccuracies than it is to rebut a complex set of philosophical beliefs. Each of us is equipped with a mental filtering system which tends to reject information that clashes with ideas that we have already accepted. However, it also tends to reject ideas from sources that we have come to regard as unreliable and admit information from reliable sources. The technique you use in your films is apparently designed to penetrate the filter by inserting information that does not meet with immediate rejection but which may generate reactions which eventually alter the filter itself. This is an intriguing approach, and I would be interested in knowing how it actually works.

The approach I have described is less sophisticated. It seeks to alter the filter by working on the part that relates to the reliability of the source of the information. If in fact the filter is adjusted to accept information from unreliable sources, there is a good chance of altering it by demonstrating that the source is unreliable. The problem here is to penetrate with information that is not rejected by the filter, either because it clashes with entrenched ideas or comes from a source that the filter automatically refuses to admit.

One of our problems today is that too many of us are too polite or too unconcerned to expose those who misrepresent the facts. Our media will frequently give as much or more time and space to outrageous liars as they give to people who try to be careful and responsible in dealing with the facts. This is the curse of sensationalism. Audiences composed of knowledgeable students, professors, and even businessmen, will sometimes sit quietly and listen to speeches made by individuals who play fast and loose with facts, and even applaud their distortion. It is not too surprising that many of our young people come to look at the world with distorted vision.

Your technique for dealing with this sounds interesting and promising. At the same time, there is a place for the direct attack.

Sincerely,

J. L. Robertson

part 8

do we worry needlessly?

AN OLD FRIEND OF MINE, Harry E. Chrisman of Denver, Colorado, wrote to me at considerable length to express a viewpoint that I am sure is shared by many adults. He reminded me that youth has always been a period for rebelliousness and some sowing of wild oats. He thought that adults were too inclined to condemn young people because of minor differences or transgressions. He suggested that we should think kindly of our youth.

I know that his views are shared by many parents who refuse to get too alarmed about the generational conflict. One sometimes hears a quotation from an ancient Greek or Roman bemoaning the fact that the younger generation is going to the dogs. One is expected to conclude from this that the older generation is always inclined to view youth with alarm but that its worries are always needless. The world goes on spinning and the human race survives.

What those who take this confident view overlook is that while the human race has survived, great nations have also fallen. Some very terrible things have befallen humanity—some of the worst of them in my own lifetime.

I pointed out in my reply to Harry Chrisman that there was a danger in being too complacent about the way things are going in America. Arthur Krock, the veteran journalist, said in his *Memoirs, Sixty Years on the Firing Line,* that he feared that America's period of glory as a great nation might be one of the briefest in history. We have no assurance from on high that we will not suffer the fate that many other peoples have endured once they abandoned or lost the key to greatness. The decline of a nation does not take place overnight. It is generally perceptible only to historians looking back over several generations. Those who perceived such a decline at the time it was taking place were the Jeremiahs whose warnings were more frequently ignored than heeded.

I found myself, in my reply to Harry, coming back to the basic idea of my Omaha speech, which started this correspondence. America is in danger if we do not take measures to preserve and protect the operational values that made this country great. We are not beyond the point of no return by any means, and I am not predicting disaster. On the contrary, I am optimistic about our future, because I believe that the American people are sound and sensible enough to see the dangers that exist in some of the present trends. I believe those trends can and will be altered.

October 7, 1969

Dear Louis:

I feel that we older folks are pretty much in the mold of our own parents, and fail to understand youth. I am of the judgment that most of the youth of today are as good or better than we were in our own time. There was always an anarchistic edge to youth, even then. I remember three or four of my good boyhood friends who sampled marijuana (they called it "hay" then) and I recall that two or three of them were later hooked on drugs. I believe all are dead today; one I remember was a Marine in WW II and laid in the Vets

Hospital for several months, a real victim of his own excesses—and folly.

But the general run of our youth were responsible fellows, and even those of us who held most unorthodox views of our contemporary society, and have been scolded and sometimes wrongly "judged" by that society, made at least ordinary citizens and avoided prison. So I take issue with you in the paragraph where you charge youth with not wanting to preserve the ideas and values that made this country great in the first place—that is, sort of lumping them in as "totalitarians." That is exactly what all responsible youth want today, and they feel their generation is being, and will be, thwarted from realizing the most of America's potential by the members of the older generation who have goofed off so badly when dealing with social reforms.

Our problems are, of course, nothing new to you and me. The country was blindly running its economic course when I was in my early twenties. It ran into the brick wall of Depression, and by some deft maneuvering escaped a revolution at that time, largely by means of another World War to start the machine running again. The youth of today blame **us** for that folly, and of course you and I and our generation are not responsible, for we inherited the social and economic system as it was at that time.

I have always thought that our generation **did well** to escape Fascism, or Naziism, and a great many of our old boyhood friends gave their lives in that cause. But all the while our leadership, particularly that in the big business circle, was pointing to "communism" as the greatest threat. I recall well how the big business interests of Germany and Italy supported the Nazi-Fascist groups in coming to power in their countries, and I fear that a great many of our businessmen in the nation would, and may, make the same mistake. For rather than yield a small bit of their power, and their gains, they would bring into focus a new terror so much

171

worse than any of us have known that I would not like to contemplate it.

I have worked in the business world all my life. I have personally talked with thousands of businessmen. So their wisdom does not awe me as it does others. Further, I have served in the military forces, and I have seen the follies of a general in his big command. So I know a little about how the military mind functions; how it thinks in terms of "requisitioning," never in terms of "how much in taxes must I pay to enjoy this new weapon."

It seems to me that our national government is clearly out of tune with the rest of the nation. I further believe that this has been so for at least 20 or more years. We have had a succession of Presidents, only one of whom was justified in being elected by some great prior service in governmental leadership. Somehow, we have been unable through our normal elective system to put forth the **best** men in the nation to the top places in government. We have, as a result, received poor leadership. Even today, we find difficulty in finding a man from **either** the Democrat or Republican party to take the high place on the Supreme Court, that is a man whose hands are not tarnished with some unethical maneuver or graft. How can it be that if these political parties are properly functioning they cannot do better than that? And this condition runs clear down into the precincts. I hear many complaints of folks about this condition on the lowest as well as the highest echelons of government, both elderly people and the young people I know.

The youth tell me that we older folks **talk** a great Democracy; but that we wouldn't recognize one if we saw it. They are very disillusioned with the effort to integrate all races, and most of them have begun to see the class structure of our society, with the rich ever getting richer, and failing to even bear their share of taxes, while the poor have become so disgusted that they just take relief and forget their woes as a democratic people. And I believe that it is this bottom strata that will pull us all down if something is not resolved in the next decade or two, work found to bring them into responsible citizenship again—that is if they have ever been there.

My wife and I help a friend's family after his death and that of his wife. They were relief kids, 16, 14, 12 and 10 in age, never had known anything else. When we began to talk about their hopes, their plans, their future, their desires to function in the society, they just had a blank stare. Down there, no one is asking them if they want to be doctors or lawyers—or sheepherders. There the talk was of a Joy World, no responsibility.

I can recall when the great battles for relief, social security, business loans and all were being fought out in the 'thirties. My people were only looking for work, not handouts. I had the feeling then, though I also worked for the better social legislation, that in this country it was not the better way. I had the feeling that if the great power of the nation was harnessed to aid all the people, it would be a more practicable way than to select particular groups, then pay them off at the expense of the rest of us. And as soon as the more wealthy interests saw how this legislation could be converted to their own personal interests, I knew it would start flowing down another channel. Too much of the relief money— whether to the biggest businesses or to the paupers—never reaches the people who need help the most.

But to get back to youth. We mistrust them because they **look so different.** Their long hair, their unkempt appearance, their clothes styles, all are as foreign to us—well, even more foreign than the clothing of a Russian communist! So we distrust them as much as we do a communist. Take this example: Last night there was a ring on the doorbell about nine o'clock. Our street here has no street lights, so it's as dark as the inside of a motorman's glove. I turned on the porch light, and answered the door, quite cautiously, I must say. Outside was a "hippy" looking boy in his teens. He asked if I had seen a "golden-haired" dog, a small puppy. I glanced out to the yard, almost expecting to see several other young fellows hiding in the deadfall from our trees, which were broken down in a 21-inch snowfall here Saturday. No others were visible. So I answered his question and he left. When my wife asked about the caller, I related his question. "Why that's the little dog that was run over down by the bank," she said. I had been driving when we passed the dog on the street that afternoon, and several used-car men were petting him as he lay on the ground there near the bank building. So we called the motel where this lad was staying; fortunately he had left his first name, "Jim." And I hope his dog lived.

But there is an example of our **distrust** of youth. This kid had lost a little pup of which he was fond. He was out trying to do something about it, rather than sit in his motel room and grieve, or ask some adult to resolve his problem. That is where youth is today, the very best ones, the kind that would have volunteered in the first American Revolution, and whose descendants would have idolized them. They are out on the streets, and on the campuses. In my time, I would have joined them, but too many of us at that time in history were bumming rides on freight trains, and had no chance to group and talk over some method for action. Well, the colleges and universities—and even the high schools—are today providing a meeting ground for youth. I smell a great change coming, whether we want it or not. If I was advising business groups today what to do, I would ask them to change their ways, **to start letting democracy function**; to get behind the desegregation movement; to give the minority peoples the same opportunities as we white gentiles have always had in this country; to curb the trend towards monopoly if they do not want socialism to become the basic issue in politics. There is still a

174

great opportunity for American free enterprise to function here in this country, if those who live it the most don't husband it **all to themselves.** . . .

Well, think kindly of our youth. They are mostly good kids, well-meaning, even those wearing leather—or black plastic—jackets, and those global helmets of the motorcycle trade! And remember: They are compelled by law in most states to wear those helmets, which make all of us think of a state policeman getting ready to pinch us for some infraction of rules, when they roar up beside us! By the way, did you see that film, "Easy Rider"? I had the feeling that it ended just right, for boys who turn themselves on into such channels of life might as well be turned off before they injure others. . . . I have the feeling that when they get down into the WHY of youngsters taking dope they will find the same reasons they found for the alcoholics; some other definable and reachable reason, buried far beneath their skin, so deep it will take a first class psychiatrist weeks to uncover it.

Like you, I hope that **patience** will remain as a virtue, particularly among our young friends. But when youth sees a 40-story apartment building erected in a few weeks, they have the feeling that other (social) problems shouldn't remain on the docket for 200 or 300 more years. Like them, I am willing to chance a change every hundred years, for I believe that people **get** the type of government they **deserve,** and we, today, are reaping where our ancestors and ourselves sowed. Well, thanks for your views. It is always good to see how old friends have moved along life's pathway in 50 or so years, and how the buffeting of the winds of chance have shaped us (just to mix a metaphor). But I am sure that all of us have at heart the better interests of this good old country that has fed and clothed us.

Sincerely,
Harry E. Chrisman
Denver, Colorado

"No parent in the country can shrug it (drugs) off as someone else's problem, because no one with children or grandchildren can rest assured that his loved ones will escape."

Dear Harry:

Your thoughtful letter came as a useful reminder that the days gone by also had their blemishes, tensions, and problems. There is a popular song about kids that asks, "Why can't they be like we were, perfect in every way?" I suppose every parent of every generation tends to succumb to that feeling at times.

But we both recognize that changes do take place. And it is not just the old fogeys who think that the changes are not always for the better.

Let's consider one specific matter you raise in your letter—the use of drugs. We surely cannot compare the experimentation that took place with marijuana fifty or even ten years ago with what we see throughout the country today. It is estimated that in New York City alone there will be 1,000 deaths caused directly by drug abuse this year, and a high percentage of these victims will be youngsters. You personally knew two or three individuals who came to a tragic end through the use of drugs when you were young. Most of us never encountered anyone who used drugs. That is not the environment that our young people find in their schools today. Drugs are being pushed in the high schools and in some communities even in the elementary schools. Can we really view this with complacency?

Of the three or four you knew who experimented with marijuana, two or three later became hooked on hard drugs. Dr. Robert W. Baird, Director of the Haven Clinic for Drug Addicts in New York City, who has had long and close experience with drug addiction, confirms that this is a common development. He states that if we were to remove the penalties against the possession and use of marijuana, a step that many of your youngsters advocate, we would end up with 1 to 1.5 million users of heroin in the United States by 1975. This,

Chrisman: *"There was always an anarchistic edge to youth. . . . I remember three or four of my good boyhood friends who sampled marijuana (they called it 'hay' then)."*

SLAVERY 1969

he says, would mean the demise of a great nation. That is not a pleasant thought to contemplate. Perhaps Dr. Baird is wrong, but the fact is that he has been consistently right in his warnings about the growth of drug use in the past. We had better pay some attention to him.

Having seen the human tragedy that drug abuse brings in its wake, I can hardly express the horror I feel when I contemplate the possible expansion of this plague that Dr. Baird foresees. I do not think we can fully appreciate what this will mean unless we place ourselves in the position of a family that has lost one of its members to drug addiction. It is heartbreaking to see a much-loved child dragged down into degradation and an early death, destroying dreams, introducing bitterness and hatred into familial relations that should be full of love, and bringing shame and remorse to all involved. It is literally true that today children are being lured into this trap at an age when they are still playing with toys. They are running away from home, wonderful homes in many cases, to join the sub-culture of the addicts before they have even finished junior high. This is a situation that we had better get excited about. No parent in the country can shrug it off as someone else's problem, because no one with children or grandchildren can rest assured that his loved ones will escape.

Imagine the lives that will be ruined, the tears that will be shed, the crimes that will be committed, if we permit addiction to develop to the level predicted by Dr. Baird. We surely did not have this hanging over our heads when you and I were young.

I plead innocent to the charge that I am condemning the younger generation *en masse*. I am sure that basically the younger generation is, for the most part, at least as good and probably better than we were in our time.

Testimony before the House Select Committee on Crime, October 15, 1969.

However, one of the habits I have had to develop as a central banker is that of keeping a sharp eye on underlying trends—not always successfully, I will admit—in order to try to detect significant changes in time to do something about them. We cannot afford to take the Pollyannish view that nothing bad can ever happen to us. The fact is that in our lifetime we have seen three great countries—Russia, Germany, and China, and many lesser countries—fall into the grip of cruel totalitarianism. When you and I were youngsters it was possible to talk about the irresistible march of democracy. If we stand back and look at our times in perspective, would we not have to admit that democracy and the liberal values associated with it have been in retreat for perhaps two decades?

I remember that back in the 'thirties there was a saying about totalitarianism: "It can't happen here." I am not so sure. Some who lived in Germany in the 'twenties and 'thirties are telling us now that there are some strong similarities between the behavior of youth there in those days and the behavior of many of our young people today. Refugees from Castro's dictatorship tell us with worried voices that they see strong similarities between the climate on many of our college campuses and the climate in Cuba that enabled Castro to seize absolute power.

I do not believe that the Russian youth in 1917, the German youth in 1933, the Chinese youth in 1949, or the Cuban youth in 1959 were basically bad. But the fact is that many of them were on the side of totalitarianism and assisted in its triumph. No doubt most of them subsequently recognized their error and regretted it. But the deed was done and the subsequent suffering and bloodshed have been incalculable.

I agree with you that we did well to escape totalitarianism in this country in the 'thirties. The Great Depression certainly gave ample reason for discontent and rebellion against the *status quo*. I believe that what saved us was the fact that 99 per cent of us, including even the recent immigrants who could not speak English, placed loyalty to America and to its basic political ideals very high in our value system. Even the communists pretended to be loyal Americans. For all the imperfections of our system, it still seemed preferable to what were called "alien" systems in those days. George Washington, Thomas Jefferson, Benjamin Franklin and Abraham Lincoln were revered as heroes, so much so that the communists named their New York school after Jefferson, and the recruits they gathered together to fight in the Spanish Civil War constituted what was called "The Abraham Lincoln Brigade."

I have noted a significant change in the last few years. In many of our schools our children are being taught that our Founding Fathers had feet of clay. I have heard that in some classes more attention is paid to their feet than to either their heads or their backbones. One does not have to look far to find those on the fringes who openly boast that they have no love for or loyalty to America. They flaunt the flag of the Vietnamese communists and publicly burn the Stars and Stripes. The enemies of free institutions no longer drape themselves in the flag and hide behind the names of Jefferson and Lincoln. They establish as their heroes totalitarians such as Che Guevara and Mao Tse-tung. A recent survey at Cornell University revealed that over a fifth of the students questioned said that they approved of violent or disruptive protests under exceptional circumstances. Another 2 per cent approved of violence as a general principle.

Ideas are the forerunners of events. I find it difficult to believe that we can have a substantial percentage of our most intellectually active young people indoctrinated with hatred for their own country and its institutions and admiration for totalitarian regimes and methods without risking some rather painful consequences.

181

The ancient Greeks noted that democracy tended to break down and give way to tyranny. First, of course, some substantial segment of the population must be conditioned to accept the idea that tyranny is preferable to democracy. We now have a substantial number of young people, some of them students and some teachers, who accept this philosophically. Their number is still relatively small, but they seem to be highly motivated and are willing to go to any extreme to impose their will on others. They have created unprecedented turmoil in our schools, and unless remedial steps are taken, I have no doubt that they will multiply their numbers and increase their trouble-making capabilities. We have seen this develop in Japan, where first the disruption was limited to part of the universities, then extended to paralyze whole institutions for long periods of time, and finally, on October 21, 1969, it spread out to produce paralysis of Tokyo, the largest city in the world, for an entire day.

I very much doubt that these youthful revolutionaries will ever succeed in imposing their dictatorship upon us—or upon Japan, for that matter. What I do fear is that their extremism will generate an overwhelming demand for protection against them, at the cost of many of our traditional liberties. The cycle noted by the Greeks will be repeated in America if democracy functions in such a way that it destroys our domestic tranquility.

Actually, it is a miracle that America has survived as a nation as long as it has. We nearly came apart at the seams during the Civil War. Lincoln, inspired by Washington's emphasis on the importance of maintaining the Union, held us together. Considering the tremendous problems engendered by that bitter conflict (in which my own father was, as you know, an active participant), the racial, ethnic and linguistic diversity, the vastness of the country, and the clash of regional economic interests, our success is quite amazing. The secret lies in our forefathers' ability to inculcate in their children and in the millions of immigrants faith in the American system. That is the cement that has bound this huge disparate collection of people into a viable and dynamic nation. If you find a solvent that will dissolve that cement, you can destroy America as we know it.

Who would want to do a thing like that?

Quite a few people, it seems. We can start with the gentlemen in the Kremlin, who in the summer of 1969 summoned their agents from sixty-nine countries or geographic entities to Moscow for a conference, where they renewed their pledge to work for the destruction of the American system. The resolutions adopted were not widely reported by the American mass media, perhaps because they did not fit in with the view popular in some circles that Moscow has long since abandoned such ideas. I need not dwell on the openly proclaimed interest that certain other foreign dictators have in our collapse. They think that they have found the solvent that will destroy the cement that binds us together, and they are applying it in liberal doses. But they need help. They need people inside America who can pour it on. They are finding them in ample numbers in many of our schools, where they prey on immaturity and intense idealism.

This is not entirely new. What is new is that we are not trying to defend ourselves against this attack. The essence of the American system is our devotion to liberty, democracy and the rule of law. Respect for the system was taught in the homes, the schools and the churches. Until relatively recently we did not believe that liberty, democracy and the rule of law could be preserved if we entrusted the education of our children to the advocates of totalitarian doctrines. We understood what the Greeks learned from experience—that unlimited liberty paved the way for the elimination of liberty. Our constitutional system was designed to give the maximum degree of liberty that was consistent with the preservation of liberty. And the degree that was consistent with that objective was variable, as Lincoln pointed out when confronted with the choice between curtailing liberty or permitting the dissolution of the Union.

I am not a fatalist. I do not think we are fated to survive as a free democratic society, nor do I think we are fated to see our system perish. What happens to the American system will depend on what we do to preserve and protect it. I, like you, do not stand in awe of the wisdom of our big businessmen. I think they do a fine job of running their business, for the most part. However, I have not perceived that they have outstanding vision when it comes to moral, social, and political problems. Saul Alinsky, a veteran radical, has been quoted as saying that he could get the capitalists to put up the money on Friday to finance a revolution on Saturday if they thought they could make a buck on Sunday, even though they knew they were going to be hung on Monday. We live in a highly specialized society, and the businessman sees his function as pretty much limited to doing his particular job. Improving the economic and social system, or saving it from destruction, is, for most of them, someone else's problem.

Whose problem is it? The answer is that it is everyone's problem, but that all too frequently means that it is no one's problem.

What concerns me is that I know that there are some very dedicated intelligent people, backed by considerable resources, who are by their own admission working to bring about the destruction of the American system. It is difficult to find just who is in charge of the defense against these efforts and what weapons and resources are at their disposal. We have no lack of intelligence. We know very well what is being done by those bent on our destruction. But we seem to have very little idea of what to do to block or counter their efforts.

That, I suggest, is what makes the difference between the situation that confronted our country fifty years ago and the situation confronting us today. Fifty years ago the efforts to bring about our dissolution were puny and poorly managed. Our defenses were strong. In recent years, the attack against us has grown stronger and our defenses have deteriorated.

We have fine young people, but we are not doing enough to help them preserve and pass on to their children our great heritage of free democratic institutions. We are permitting them to be confused, as many of the letters I have received in recent months show, by poorly founded accusations against our system, by unrealistic explanations of why we have not yet reached Utopia, and by an almost complete lack of understanding of conditions in some of the countries that are held up as models of social, economic, and political justice.

If we permit this to continue, we will be serving these youngsters very badly. They will end up with a far worse form of government than they deserve, and it will really be our fault, not theirs.

With best regards, I am

Sincerely,

J. L. R.

part 9

conclusion

By way of conclusion, I need say very little. The correspondence must speak for itself. All I want to add is a wish that mankind will never be satisfied with maintenance of the *status quo*. Change is always in the wind. Our efforts should be designed to make sure that changes are in the direction of progress, not retrogression.

By this time Americans must be sufficiently enlightened to avoid tearing down our form of government or our society, with only a hope that it will be replaced by something better. Surely we do not want a repeat performance of either the French revolution or the Russian one. To achieve a better nation and a better world, we must strive as dispassionately as possible to solve our problems and perfect our economic, political, and social institutions—not destroy them. Only by facing up to the problems confronting us, engaging in dialogues with concerned people of all generations, and bringing reason to bear, can we hope to prepare an unemotional climate in which good solutions can germinate, develop, and grow.

about
the author

It might seem surprising for a banker to speak out on such subjects as campus revolts, but not to those who know James Louis Robertson, Vice Chairman of the Board of Governors of the Federal Reserve System. He is acclaimed widely as an independent thinker who is as articulate as he is knowledgeable.

One of the most famous native sons of Broken Bow, Nebraska, Mr. Robertson attended Grinnell College, then received his A.B. and LL.B degrees from George Washington University. His graduate work was at Harvard Law, from which he received his LL.M. In 1964 he added his LL.D from Grinnell.

He began his government career with the Post Office, later became a special agent of the Federal Bureau of Investigation.

In 1933 he joined the legal staff of the Office of the Comptroller of the Currency during the depths of the Depression. His skill and expertise helped solve problems arising during the Bank Holiday.

Mr. Robertson served in the U.S. Naval Reserve in 1943-44. He then was appointed Deputy Comptroller of the Currency until he took office as a member of the Board of Governors of the Federal Reserve System in 1952. He is an expert on banking structure as well as on delicate monetary policies.

His reappointment in 1964 was one of President Johnson's most popular decisions—the subject of many editorials praising his selection of this outstanding independent. In March 1966 he was designated by President Johnson to serve a four-year term as Vice Chairman of the Board of Governors, and by President Nixon to serve a second four-year term, beginning March 1, 1970. In January 1969 Mr. Robertson received the Treasury Department Distinguished Service Award.

This tall, lanky Nebraskan is a voracious reader—a hobby which frequently gives information overlooked by many, and makes him more attuned to the popular side of economic problems. He plays squash and tennis as strenuously as he writes his dissents. He is constantly in demand as a speaker—not just for his knowledge of banking. *The American Banker* said of James Louis Robertson, "His ability to turn a phrase, whether in a speech or in a weighty merger decision is renowned!"

Mr. Robertson is married, and has three sons. At this writing, they range in age from 22 to 34. Alan, the youngest, is a student; Frederick is a U.S. government employee; and the eldest, James, is engaged in international private enterprise.

index

ILLUSTRATIONS